I0559483

Cello

The Magic of Music Theory

Pre-Reading A

Kristin Campbell

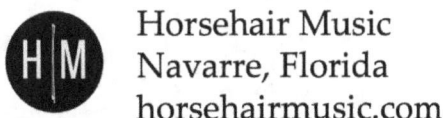

Horsehair Music
Navarre, Florida
horsehairmusic.com

Pre-Reading A Violin: ISBN 978-1-959514-06-0; Library of Congress Number: 2024907507
Pre-Reading A Viola: ISBN 978-1-959514-07-7; Library of Congress Number: 2024907535
Pre-Reading A Cello: ISBN 978-1-959514-08-4; Library of Congress Number: 2024907540

This book is dedicated to Laura Crawford and Charles Regauer, directors of the Centenary Suzuki School in Shreveport, Louisiana. Thank you for welcoming me into your Suzuki family and giving me a platform to teach theory to string students.

Special thanks to Ruth Coleman for her editorial help. Thank you to Zach Nelson for his help with the cello aural skills recordings. A big thank you to all the students who have tested out these pages and activities.

Graphics:
Cover Design: Christiana Hudson and Kristin Campbell
Hand image by www.vectorportal.com
Violin, viola, cello, bass, fingerboard and bow graphics copyright © 2024 Kristin Campbell.
All other images are in the public domain from www.freesvg.com

To the student:

Welcome to the Magic of Music Theory! Did you know that when you write things on paper it helps you remember them? This book is to help you remember things that you have learned in your lesson about your cello. This book will help you learn how to read and write music. Your practice partner will help you read and do each lesson. If you have any questions, be sure to ask your teacher. When you finish this book, you will know and understand more about your cello and playing music. It's the magic of music theory!

To the practice partner:

You are the cello hero. Practicing isn't always fun, and it's not always easy. But in this journey of learning to play the cello, you get to walk alongside a child and give them the gift of music that will last for their lifetime.

My hope with this series is that it helps you create happy memories as you work through the book. Playing games, reading stories, coloring, listening to music, learning how to draw and write notes. Depending on age and reading ability, you may need to read the pages to the student. You can learn along with them. Don't be afraid to help and lead the student to the answer. These might be new concepts and your child may not grasp it the first time it is introduced. That's ok! You will find a lot of review built in throughout the book and they will begin to understand and learn.

Keep theory time short! You can choose to do the lesson at the end of one practice session, or you could choose to divide it up with just a minute each day. Be sure and ask your teacher if they would like to do the "What Do You Hear?" pages in the lesson, or if you should access the online videos. Enjoy your journey into the magic of music theory.

To the teacher:

I created this series because I realized that my students needed some basic skills before we started note reading. I use this pre-reading series introduces students to rhythm notes, dynamic symbols, up and down on the fingerboard and the page before beginning note reading.

The aural skills pages "What Do You Hear?" can be done in the lesson or through links to online videos. Suggested recordings are linked for coloring pages, but feel free to select your favorite artist or recording to share with your student.

The Magic of Music Theory Series Guide

Use this chart to help find the level that is right for your student.

Ages 4-6 Early Book 1		Ages 6-7 Late Book 1	Ages 6-8 Early Book 2
Pre-Reading A	**Pre-Reading B**	**Primer**	**Book 1**
• Student has been playing the violin for a couple months and has learned Twinkle, Twinkle Little Star • Parent guides the student through the workbook. • Student can write English alphabet letters. • Student is not ready to read staff notation. • After completion move to Pre-Reading B.	• Student has completed Pre-Reading A. • Student knows D & A string fingerboard notes. • Student recognizes basic rhythm symbols. • Parent guides the student through the workbook. • Student can write the English alphabet letters. • After completion student will be ready to begin learning staff notes. • After completion move to Primer.	• Student is reading books at GRL level A–D. • Student is ready or has begun note reading. • Student can draw all letters of alphabet. • Primer level covers all the concepts in Pre-Reading A and B, and introduces staff notes for 2 upper strings. • After completion move to Book 1.	• Student is reading books at GRL level D–H. • Student is reading staff notes for upper 2 strings. • Book 1 covers all the concepts in Pre-Reading books and Primer and introduces staff notes for D and G strings. • After completion move to Book 2.

Table of Contents

Lesson 1

There are 4 different instruments in the string family, the violin, viola, cello and double bass.

The **violin** is the smallest member of the string family, and it plays highest notes. A person who plays the violin is called a violinist.

The **viola** is pronounced "vee-oh-la." The viola is a little bigger than the violin and plays lower notes than the violin. A person who plays the viola is called a violist [vee-oh-list].

The **cello** is pronounced "chello." The cello plays low notes. And a person who plays the cello is called a cellist [chell-ist.]. A cellist sits down to play and rests the cello between his knees.

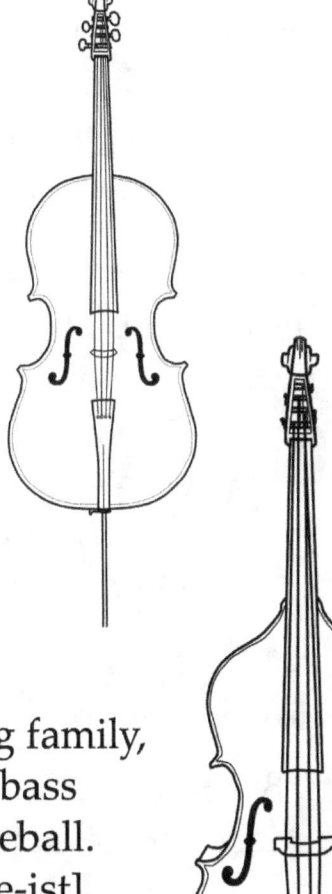

The **double bass** is the largest member of the string family, and it plays the lowest notes. Sometimes we call it bass for short. We pronounce this word "base," like baseball. A person who plays the bass is called a bassist[base-ist]. A bassist can stand up to play or sit on a tall stool to play.

Lesson 2

The 3 Bears Visit the Music Store

Once upon a time, in a big woods, lived 3 bears – a Papa Bear, a Mama Bear and a Baby Bear. One morning as Mama Bear was cooking their breakfast porridge, she said to Baby Bear, "Would you like to learn to to play a stringed instrument?" "Sure," said Baby Bear. "That sounds like fun. I like listening to string music on my tablet!" "Well," said Mama Bear, "while we wait for our porridge to cool let's go visit the music store!"

So, Papa Bear, Mama Bear and Baby Bear all went into town to *Goldie's Music Store*. "I'm so sorry that Goldie is not here today. She just left to go for a walk in the woods," said the man behind the counter. "Could I help you?" he asked. His name tag said, "Goldie's Grand Staff – My Strow." "Well, My Strow," said Papa Bear, "Baby Bear was wanting to learn to play an instrument. But on our way here, Mama Bear and I were talking and decided that we want to learn to play too. Can you help us find the right instruments?" "I would love to help you!" said My Strow.

My Strow got a violin down from the wall and handed it to Papa Bear. "Papa Bear, would you like to try a violin?" Papa Bear put the violin under his chin. When he held the violin, it looked like a little, toy in his big paws. "Wow! This is very small!" said Papa Bear. Then, he put the bow on the string. "This violin makes very high sounds. I don't think I like these high notes." "Ok. No problem," said My Strow. "Why don't you try this viola? It's a little bit bigger and sounds a little lower." Papa Bear took the viola and tried it. "Why yes, this is better. It isn't as high as the violin. But you know, when I talk my voice is very low. I like low sounds. Is there an instrument that make low sounds?" My Strow smiled and answered, "Oh yes! I know just the one! Come sit in this chair and try this cello. To play the cello, rest it between your legs." Papa Bear sat down and played some of low tones on the cello. He had a big smile and said, "Oh yes! I love this sound! This cello is *just* right!" said Papa Bear.

2. Listen to the cello play "The Swan" by Camille Saint-Saëns while you color the picture below.

Lesson 3

My Strow turned to Mama Bear. "Would you like to try playing a cello too?" "Sure," said Mama Bear. So, she sat down and played some notes. "Hmm. I liked it when Papa Bear played the low notes, but the cello sounds just a little too low for me. I'm a Mama Bear, but I really don't like to growl very much."

"Hmmm," said My Strow. "If the cello sound is too low, then you won't like the double bass sound either The bass sounds even lower than the cello!" "And," said Mama Bear "don't you have to stand up to play the bass? I'm not sure that would be very good for my back. I think my back legs would get very tired while I was practicing!" "Ok," said My Strow, "I think we agree that the double bass is not a good fit for you."

My Strow asked, "Would you like to try a violin?" Mama Bear tried playing some notes on the violin. "Oh dear, I'm sorry I'm being so picky," said Mama Bear, "but I don't really like this one either. This violin makes very high sounds, and it feels so small!" My Strow smiled and said, "No problem, Mama Bear. I know just the instrument for you! My Strow picked up a viola and handed it to Mama Bear. She took the viola and put it under her jaw. "Oh, this one feels very good. It is not quite as small as the violin." Then she began to use the bow on the strings. "These notes don't sound so low like the cello. But they aren't high like the violin either. It seems that they are right in the middle. And this viola sound so mellow and soothing. These are just the kind of sounds busy Mama Bears need to hear." Mama Bear sighed and said, "These are beautiful sounds. This viola is *just* right!"

2. Listen to the viola play Capriccio in C Minor, Op. 55 by Henri Vieuxtemps while while you color the picture below.

Lesson 4

"Now it's your turn Baby Bear," said My Strow. Baby Bear said, "Can I try the cello? I really liked it when Papa Bear played it. I try and growl as low as can " So, Baby Bear sat down and My Strow brought a small cello over for him to try. As Baby Bear tried playing the cello he said, "Well, maybe this isn't the one for me. The cello sounds a little too low for me. I don't want to try the double bass because My Strow said, that the double bass is the lowest of all the stringed instruments." "And" said My Strow "You might want to grow a little bit taller before you try playing a bass."

My Strow thought for a minute then said, "Let's try a viola like your mom." My Strow brought over a viola. Baby Bear tried the viola and said, "I like the high sounds more than the low sounds this viola makes."

"Well," My Strow said, "Maybe you should try the violin! I think I have one that is your size." He brought over a little violin. My Strow had Baby Bear put the violin under his jaw and stretched out his arm. The violin rested by his wrist. "Oh my!" said Mama Bear. "Is it too small?" "No not at all!" said My Strow "A bigger violin would make Baby Bear tired when he plays. This end of the violin that is by his paw is called the scroll. Baby Bear's paw should reach just a little past the scroll. It means this violin is the right size for him!" Baby Bear tried the bow on the strings and heard the high sounds "Oh," Baby Bear said, "This one has high notes! I love it so much!" Papa Bear and Mama Bear looked at each other and smiled. Baby Bear looked at My Strow and said, "This violin is *just* right!"

My Strow made sure they had rosin and cleaning cloth in their cases. "Well," said Papa Bear, "We all have our instruments now. Thank you for your help, My Strow!" "Glad I could help out," said My Strow. Then, the three Bears picked up their cases and headed home. "Hopefully our porridge is cool by now," said Mama Bear. "I'm starving!" said Baby Bear. "You are always hungry," said Papa Bear. The three bears sighed happily. They were headed home to practice and everything was *just* right!

THE END

2. Listen to the violin play Caprice Op. 1, No. 5 by Niccolo Pagani while you color the picture below.

What do you hear? #1

You will hear 3 notes. If the notes you hear are high, color the bird. If the notes you hear are low, color the dog.

1	2	3

You will hear 3 notes. If the notes you hear are loud, color the roaring hippo. If the notes you hear are soft, color the frog.

4	5	6

The teacher may choose from these examples. For questions 4 – 6, add a dynamic *f* or *p*.

14

Lesson 5

1. Point to each part and say its name. Using your cello, point to each part and say its name.

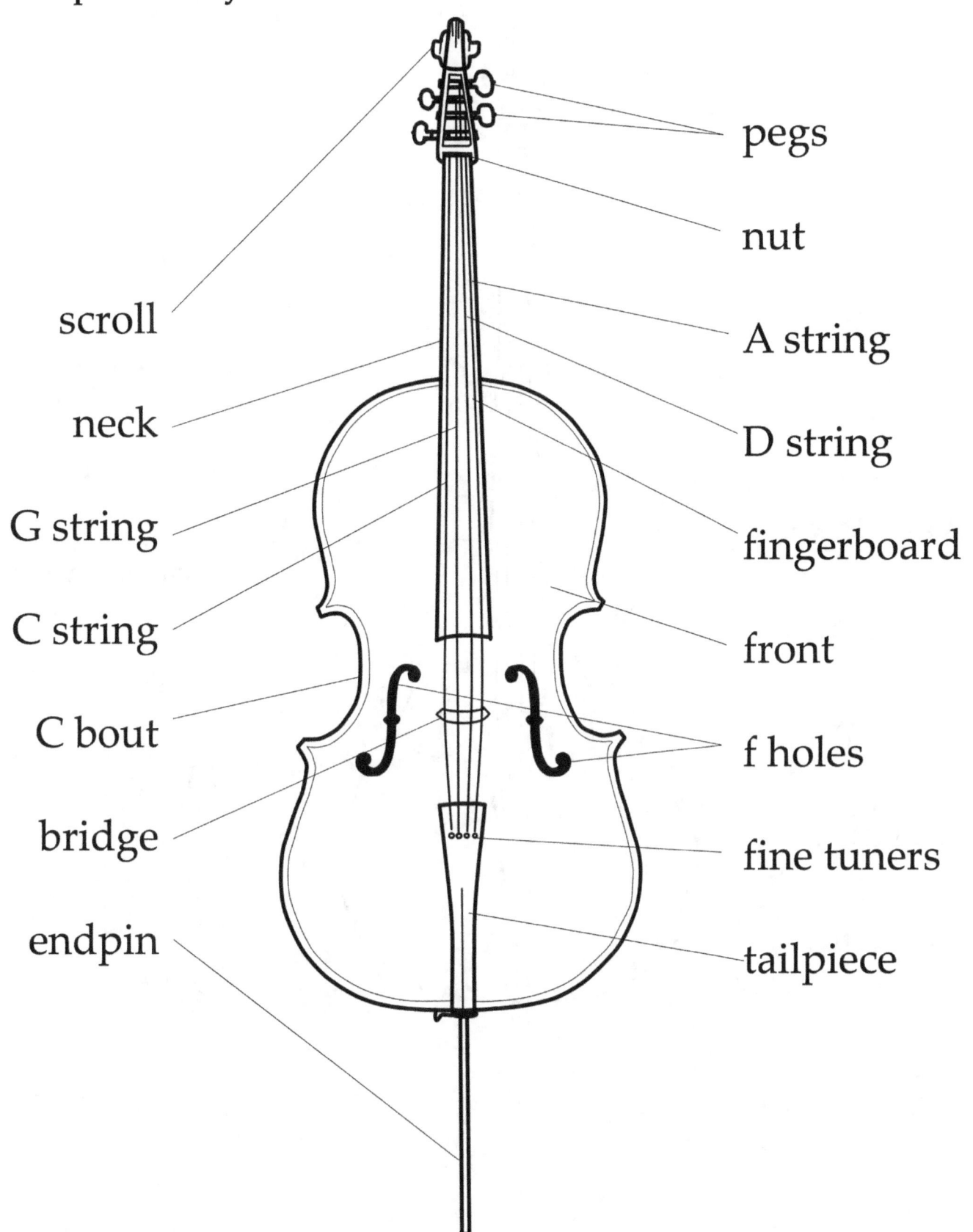

scroll

neck

G string

C string

C bout

bridge

endpin

pegs

nut

A string

D string

fingerboard

front

f holes

fine tuners

tailpiece

2. Draw a line from the word to the correct part of the cello.

pegs

nut

scroll

A string

neck

D string

G string

fingerboard

C string

front

C bout

f holes

bridge

fine tuners

endpin

tailpiece

Lesson 6

1. **Point to each part of the bow and say its name. Using your bow, point to each part and say its name.**

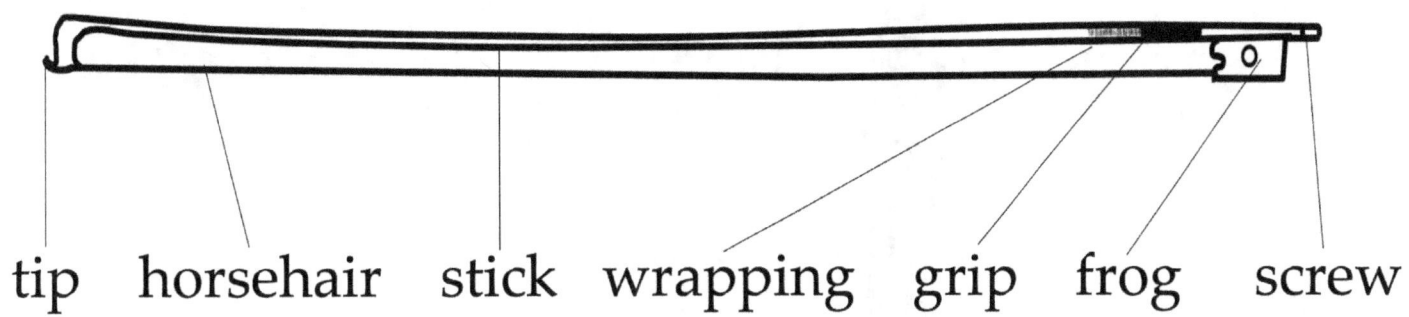

tip   horsehair   stick   wrapping   grip   frog   screw

2. **Draw a line from the word to the correct part of the bow.**

frog   tip   horsehair   grip   stick   wrapping   screw

3. **Circle the correct name for each instrument.**

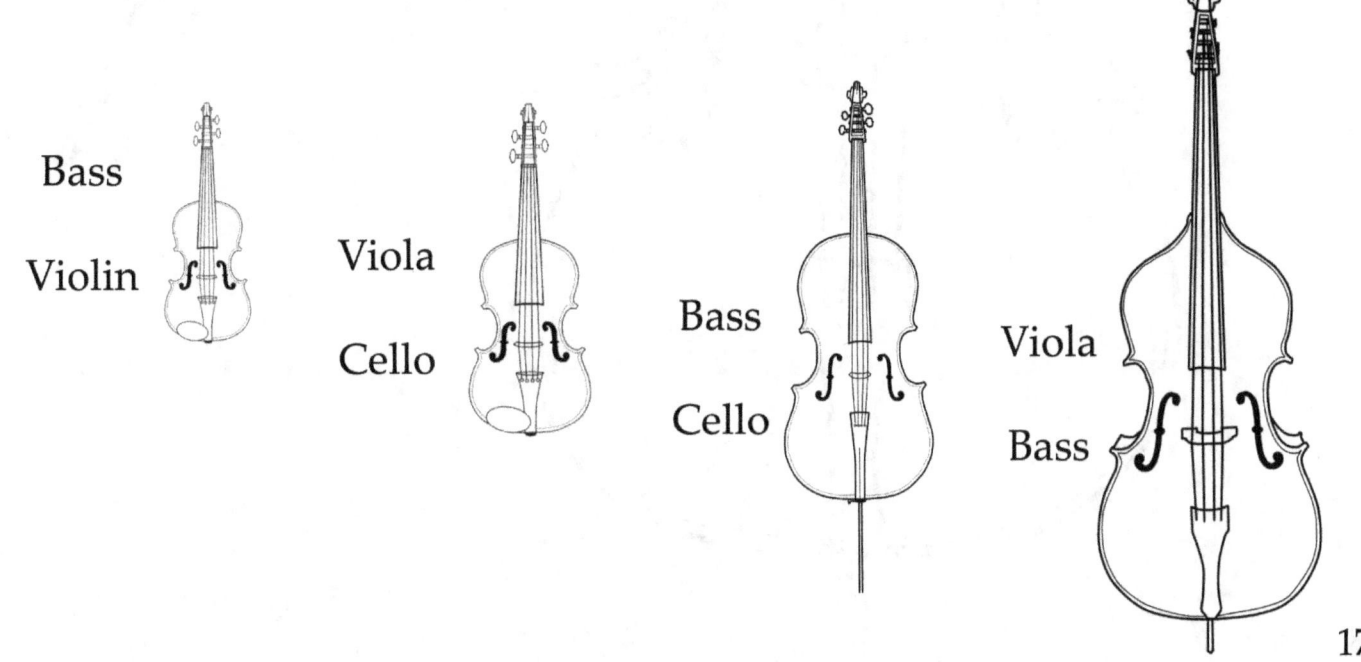

Bass

Violin

Viola

Cello

Bass

Cello

Viola

Bass

17

2. Listen to the double bass play Iberique Penisulaire by Francois Rabbath while you color the picture below.

Lesson 7

The music alphabet uses the first 7 letters of the English alphabet. There is no H in the music alphabet! When we get to G we start over at A.

1. Write one letter of the music alphabet in each oval.

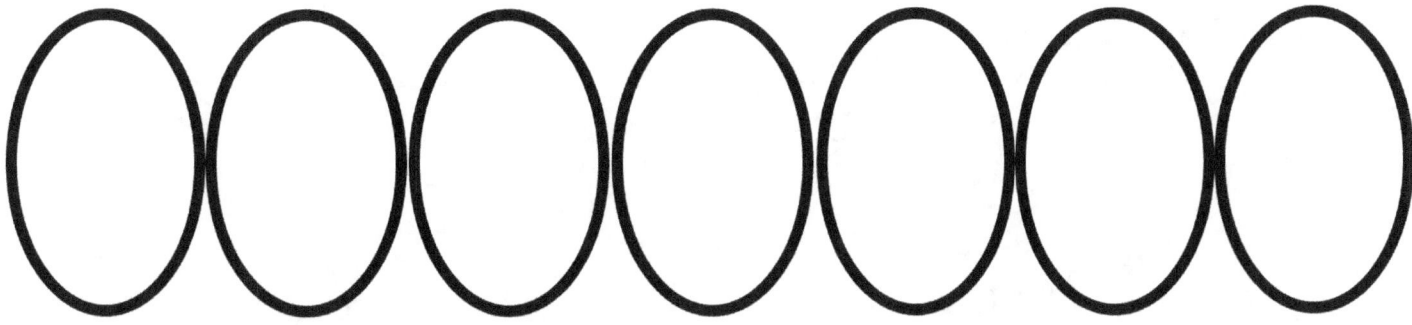

2. Say the music alphabet 2 times. Your practice partner will point while you say the letter.

3. Write in the missing letter in the empty blocks.

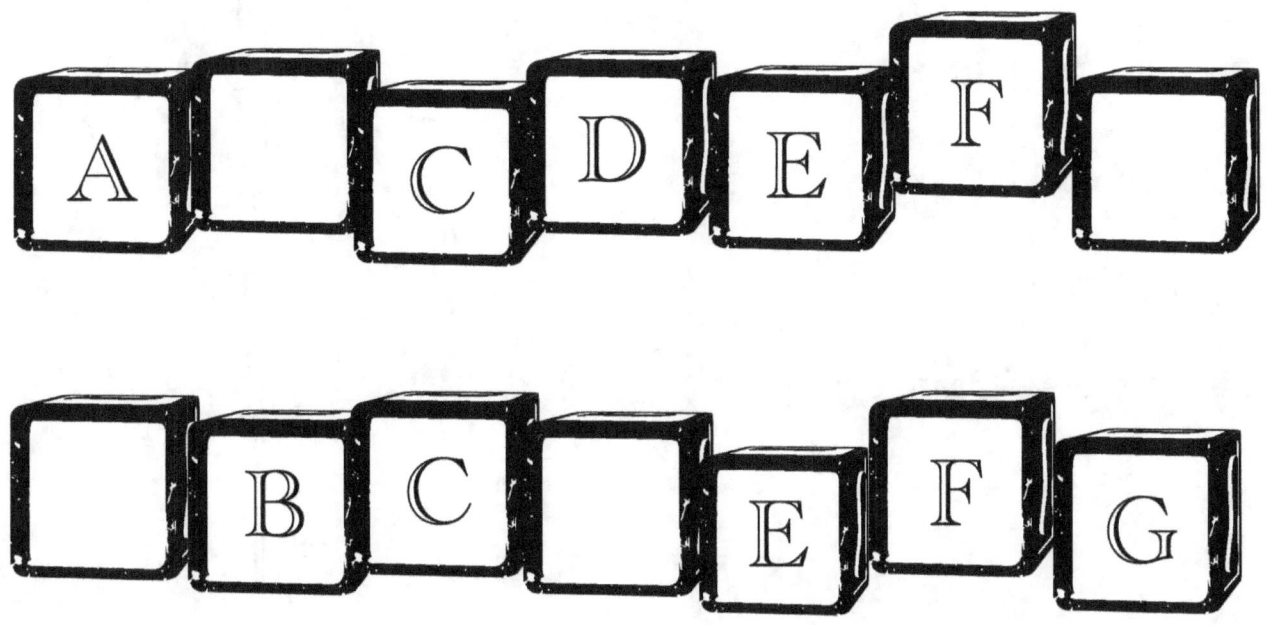

4. Draw an X through the bubbles that have the wrong music alphabet.

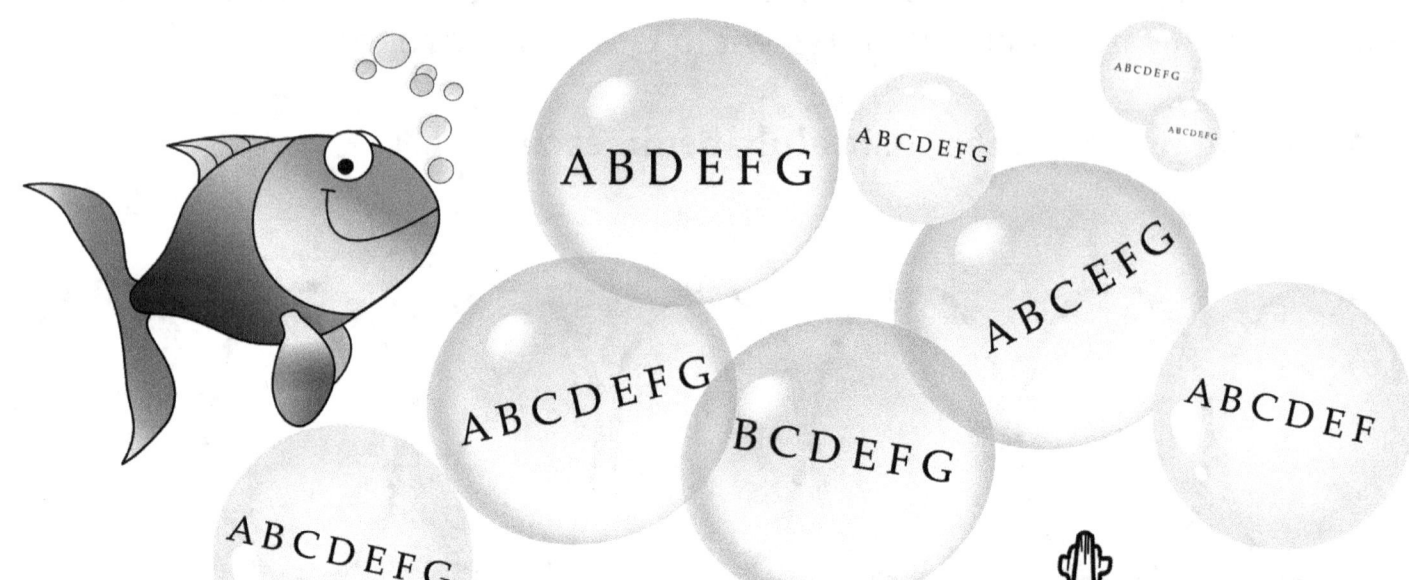

5. Color each part of the cello.

Scroll – Purple

Front – Green

Tailpiece – Red

Endpin– Dark Blue

Fingerboard – Pink

Pegs – Yellow

Fine Tuners – Orange

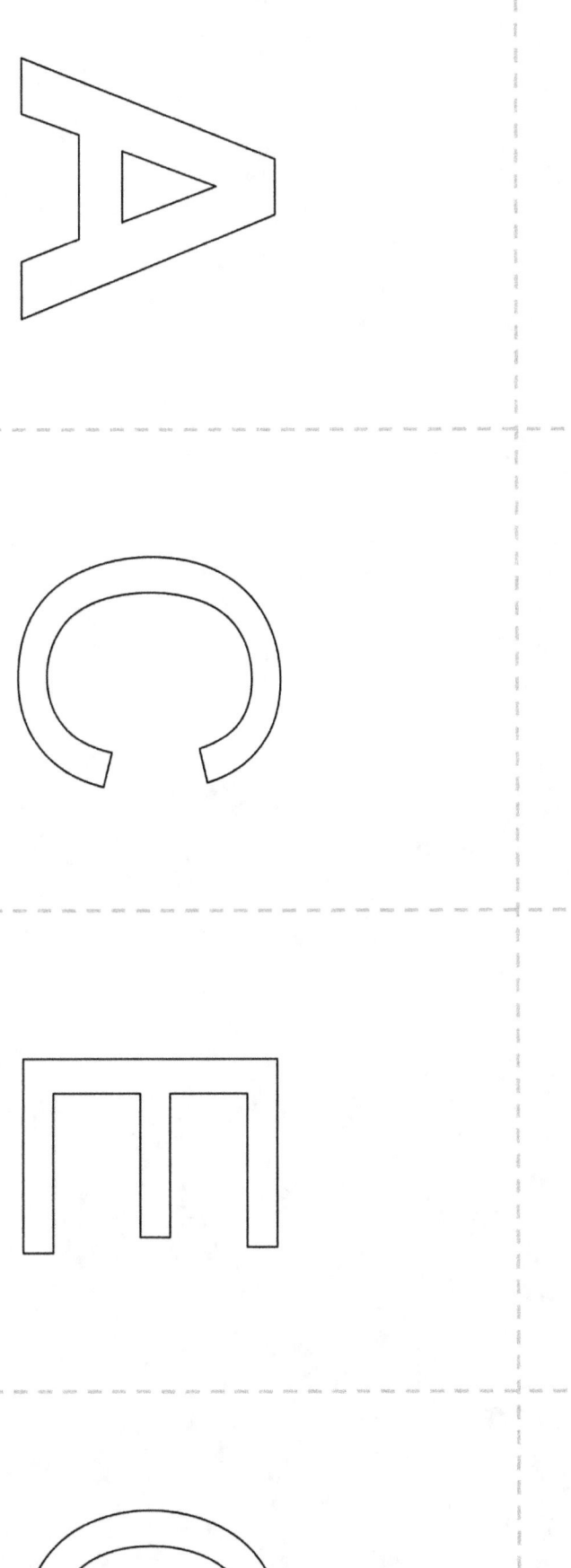
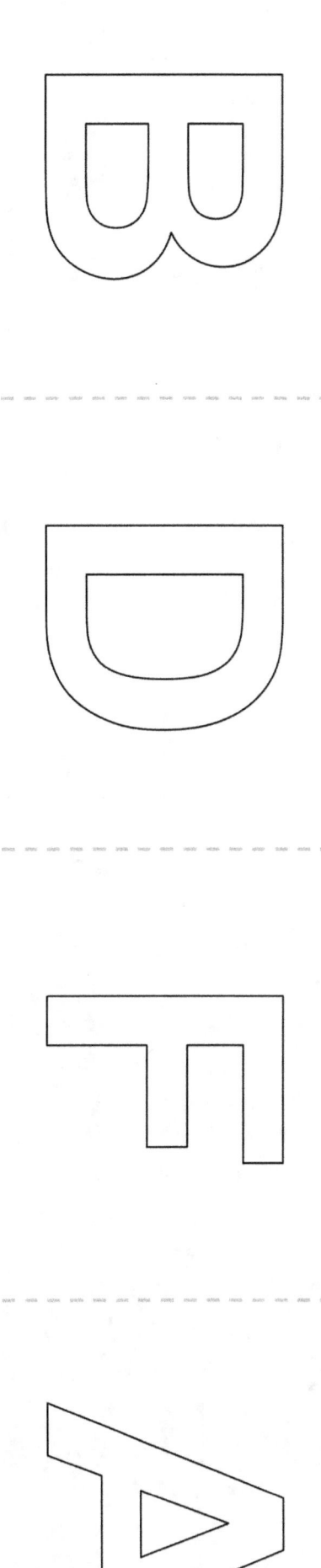
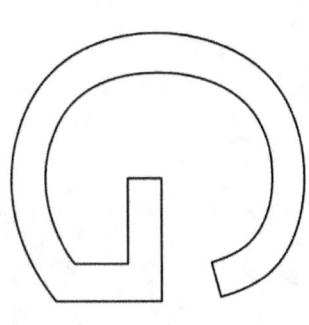
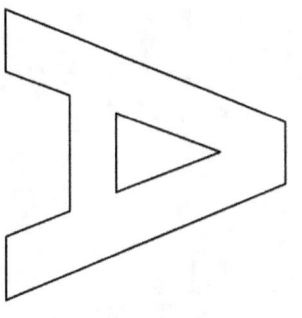

Music Alphabet Card Games

2 Players – Student and Practice Partner or Teacher

What you need:
   Tear out page 21
   Cut the along the dotted lines.

Alphabet Mix-Up

- Mix all the cards up and have the student put the alphabet in the correct order.

Who Is Missing?

- Place the cards in front of the student in order.
- Have the student close their eyes while the teacher/practice partner turns one card face down.
- Then the student opens their eyes and identifies the hidden letter.

Find the Neighbors!

- Place all the cards face up, mixed up to the side.
- The teacher/practice partner chooses one card and places in front of the student.
- The student must find and place the neighbor alphabet cards on either side of the give card.

What do you hear? #2

You will hear 3 notes. If the notes you hear are high, color the cloud. If the notes you hear are low, color the flowers.

The Magic of Music Theory Pre-Reading A · © 2024 Horsehair Music. Photocopying prohibited.

1	2	3

You will hear 3 notes. If the notes you hear are loud, color the howling dog. If the notes you hear are soft, color the cat.

4	5	6

The teacher may choose from these examples. For questions 4 – 6, add a dynamic *f* or *p*.

Lesson 8

1. The fingers on the left hand touch the strings, and the fingers on the right hand hold the bow.

Left Hand

Right Hand

2. Each finger on the left hand has a number except for the thumb. On your hand wiggle the finger that your teacher or practice partner says!

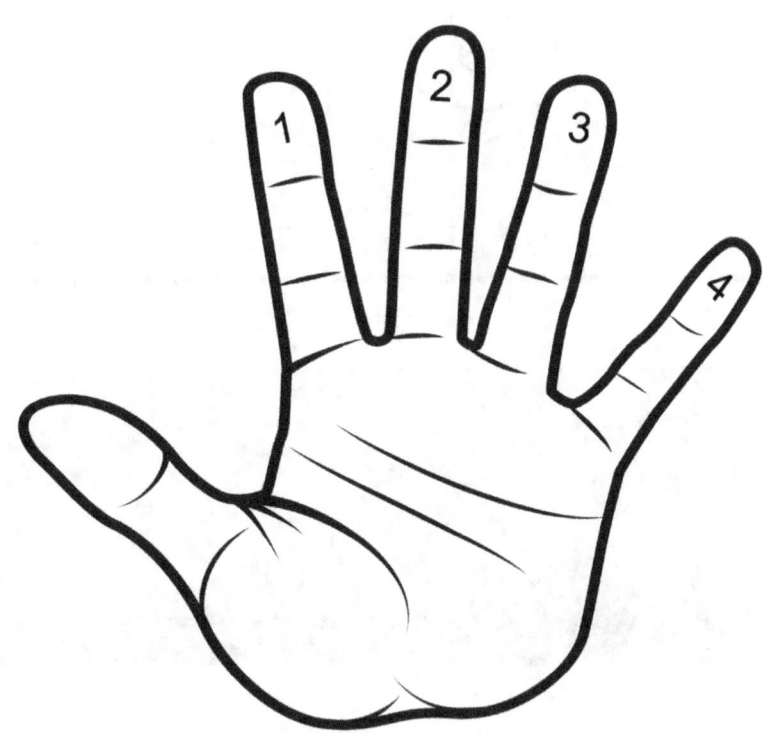

3. Place a pom-pom on each item in the vending machine. Use the finger on the tag below each item and gently pick up the pom-pom between the thumb and correct to place it in the tray at the bottom.

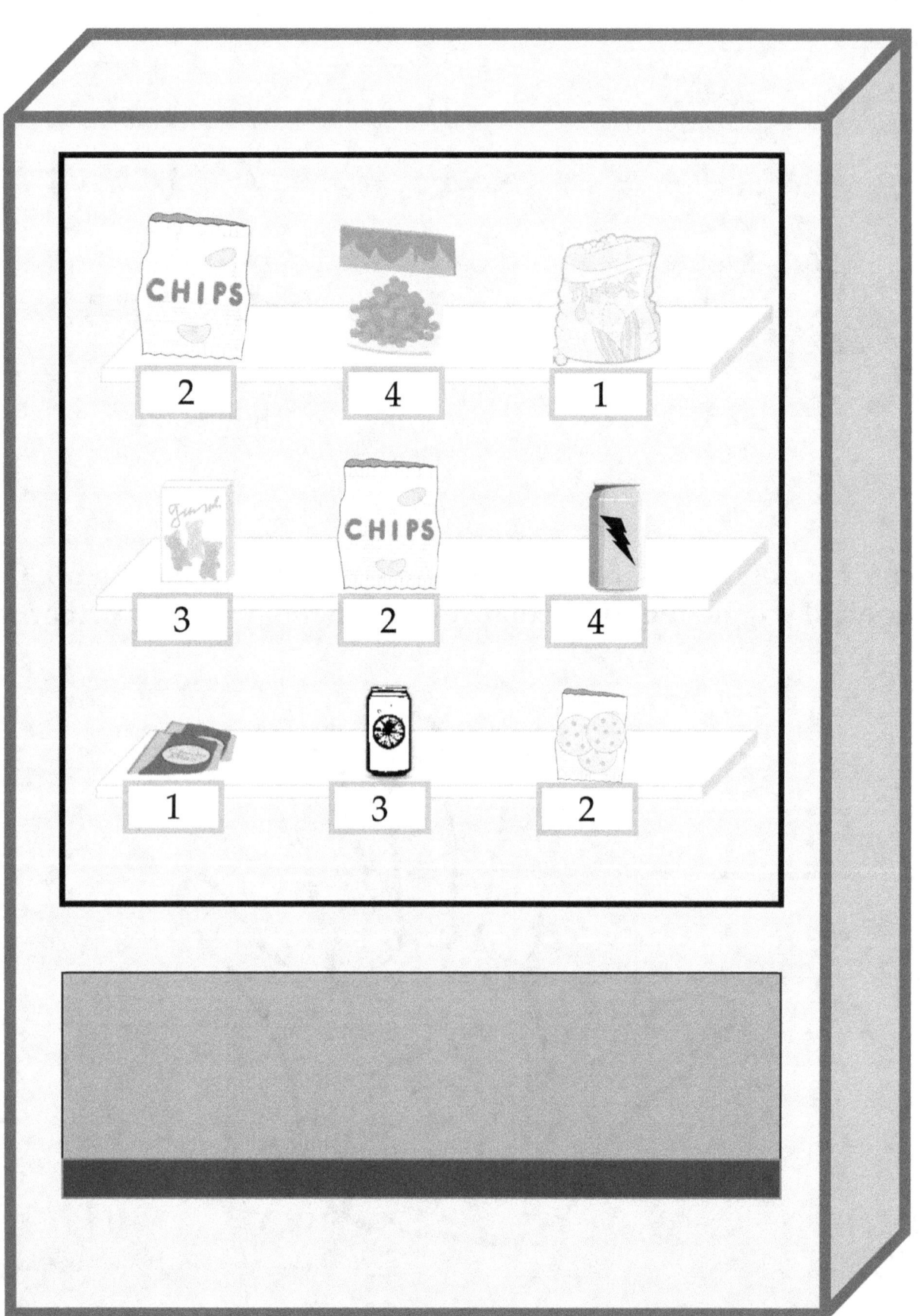

Lesson 9

1. Circle the correct hand.

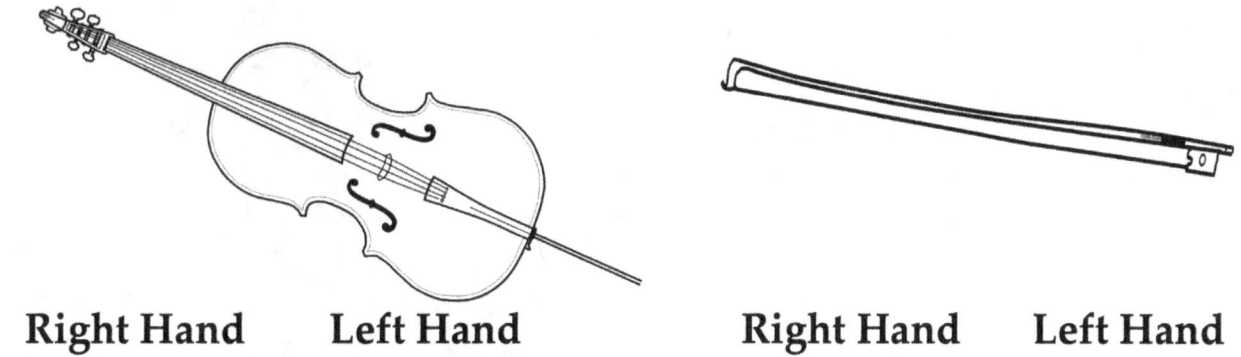

Right Hand   Left Hand   Right Hand   Left Hand

2. Write the missing music alphabet letter in the box.

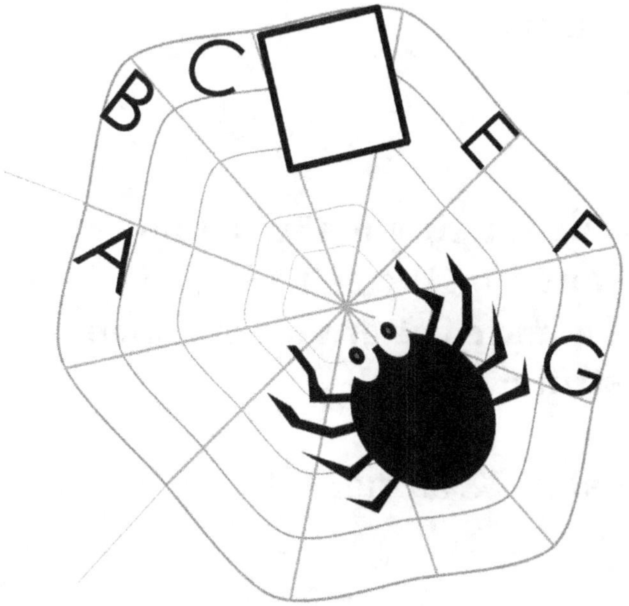

Did you know that the music alphabet lives on the cello? Each string has a letter name from the music alphabet. The string on the left is C. The C string is the lowest sounding string. Next to the C string is the G string. It sounds a little higher than the C string. The D string is next to the G string and the D string is higher than the G string. The A string is on the far right, and it makes the highest sound of all the strings on the cello.

3. Write the letters the correct house.

4. The C string makes the lowest sound on the cello. Play a Twinkle pattern on the open C string.

5. The A string makes a high sound on the cello. Play a Twinkle pattern on the open A string.

Did you hear that the A string was higher that the C string?

Lesson 10

1. Color each part of the bow the correct color.

Tip – Red	Screw – Purple
Frog – Green	Horsehair - Yellow
Stick – Blue	Wrapping – Orange

2. Color each finger the correct color.

Thumb – Red

Finger 1 – Blue

Finger 2 – Green

Finger 3 – Orange

Finger 4 – Yellow

3. Circle the instrument that matches the sentence.

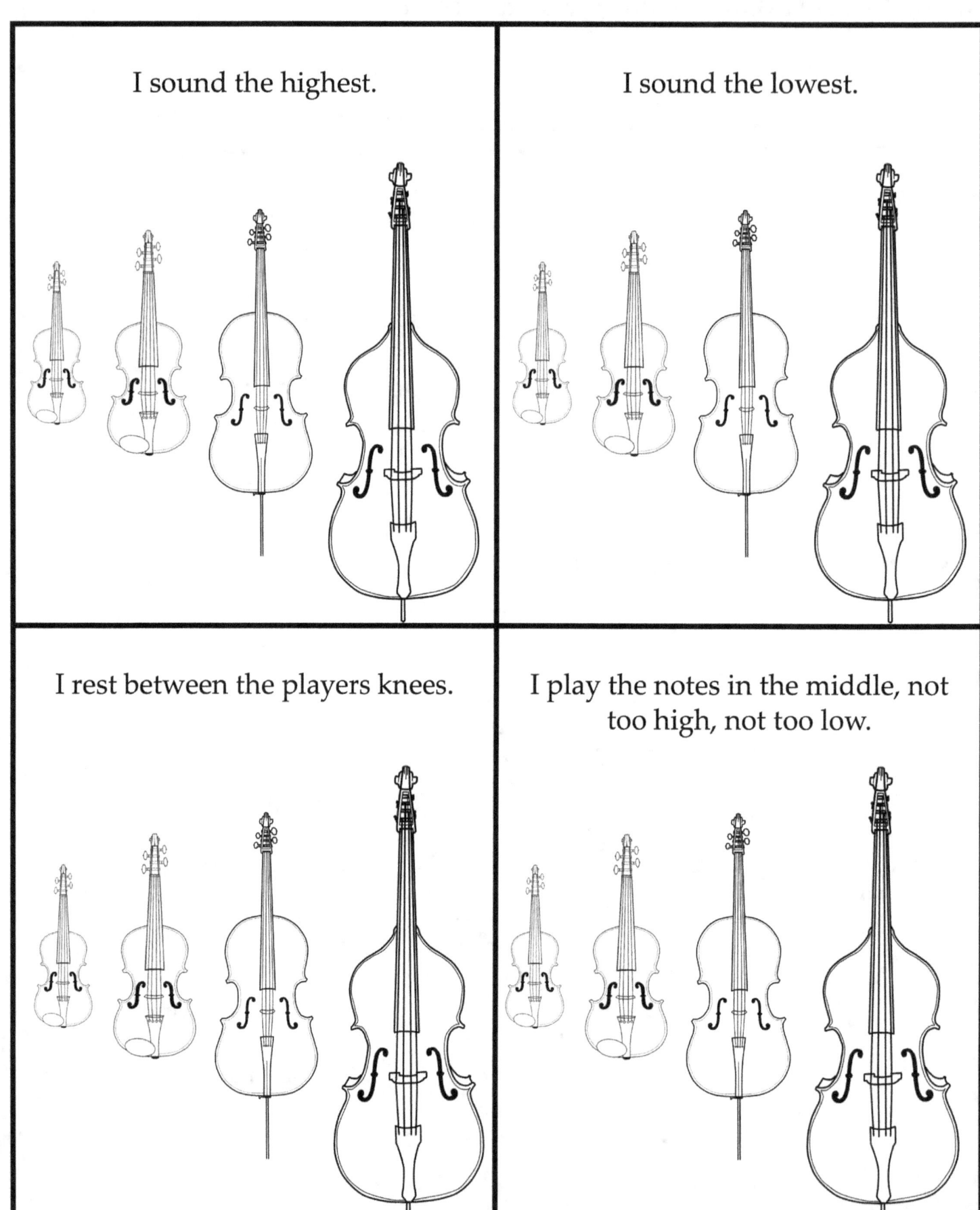

I sound the highest.

I sound the lowest.

I rest between the players knees.

I play the notes in the middle, not too high, not too low.

What do you hear? #3

If you hear low C string, circle C. If you hear the high A string, circle A.

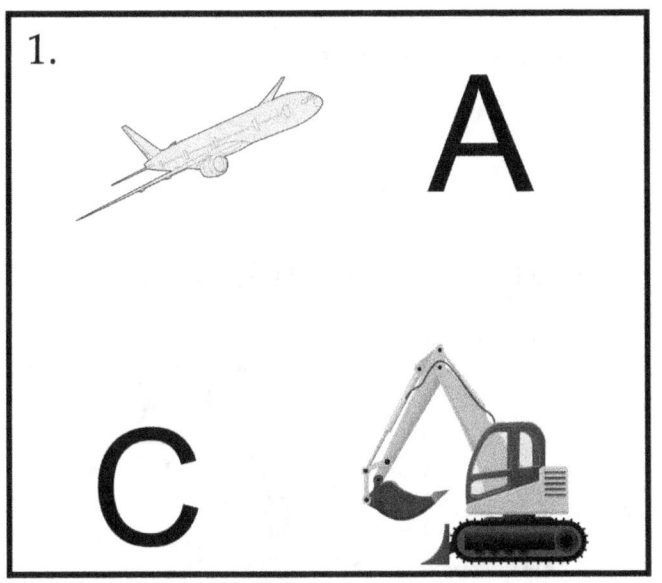

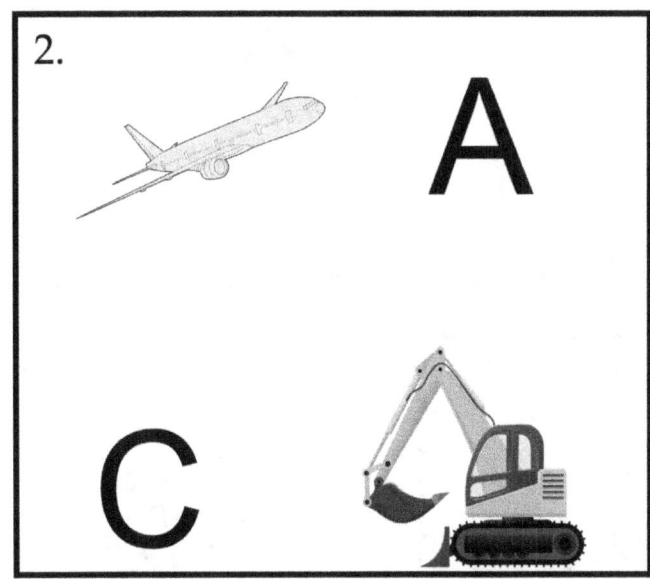

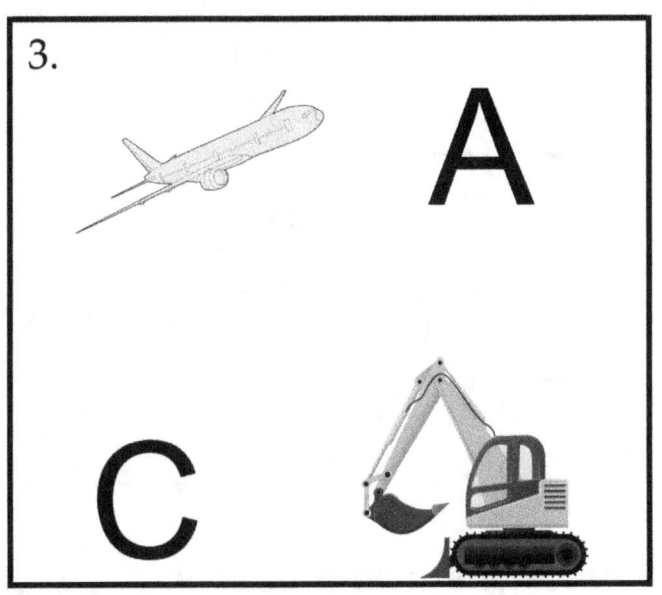

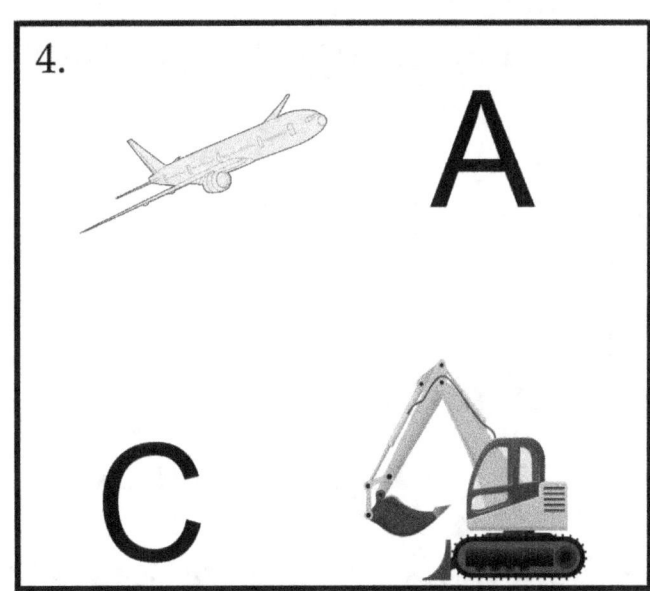

The teacher may choose from these examples:

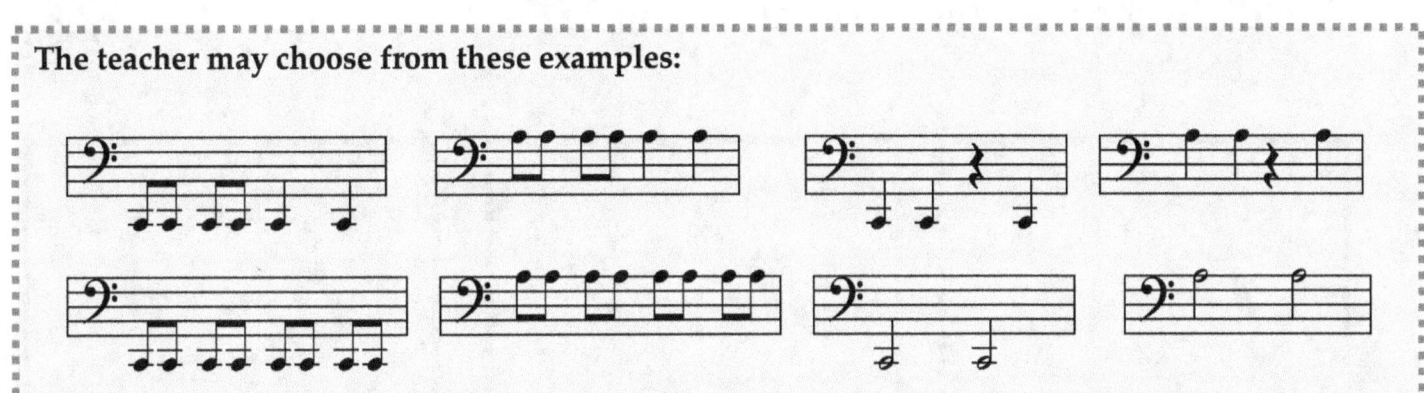

Lesson 11

Dynamics tell us the volume, how loud or soft, to play. In music the dynamics are written using Italian words. In Italian, **forte** [for-tay] means loud and **piano** [pee-an-o] means soft. Rather than write out the whole word, we use the first letter of each word to tell us what dynamic to play.

f = *forte* p = *piano*

LOUD   soft

1. Write an f or a p in the box to show what each animal is doing.

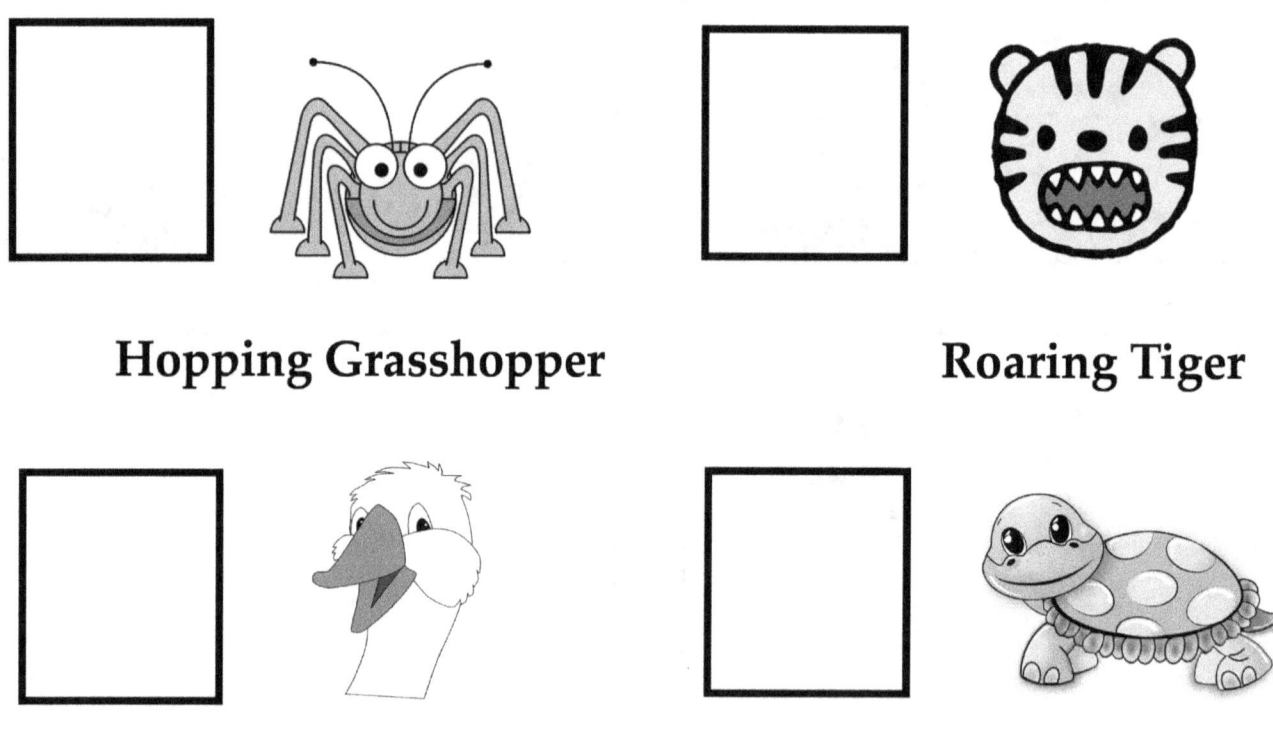

Hopping Grasshopper   **Roaring Tiger**

Quacking Duck   **Crawling Turtle**

2. You will hear 3 notes. Circle f if the notes you hear are forte. Circle p if the notes you hear are piano.

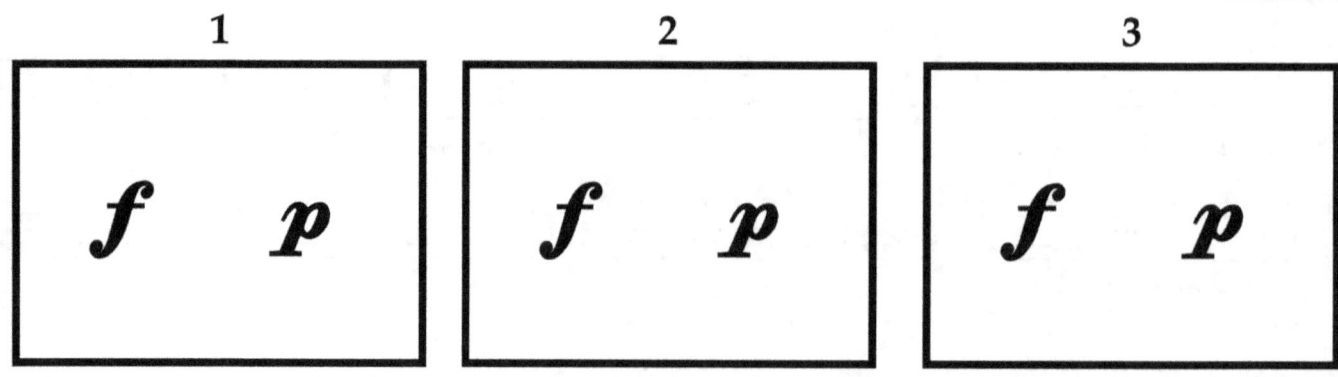

1   2   3

f p f p f p

Lesson 12

1. Write the finger numbers on each finger.

2. Write the finger numbers on the curved fingers.

3. The music alphabet blocks are mixed-up! Write the music alphabet in order starting with A. What letter comes after G in the music alphabet?

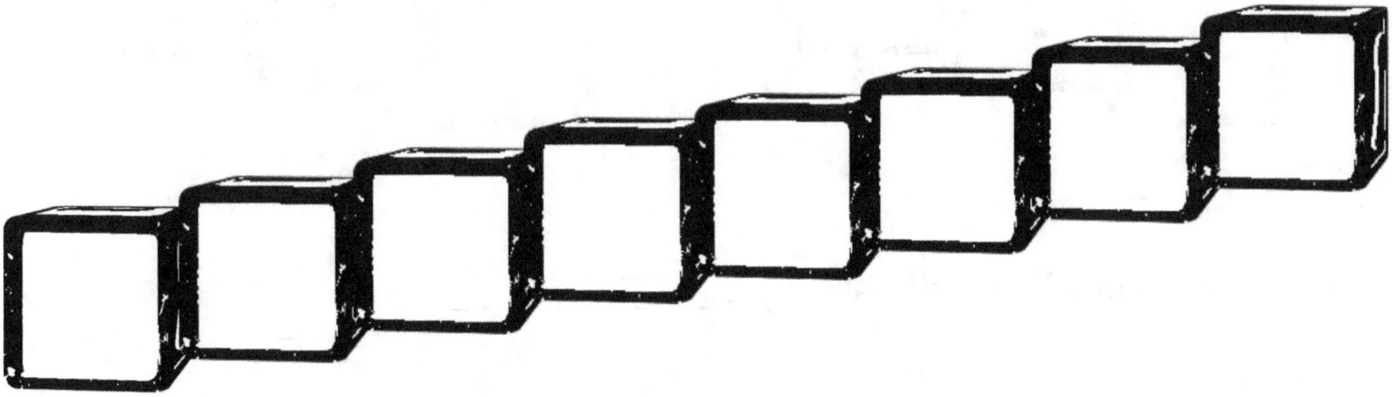

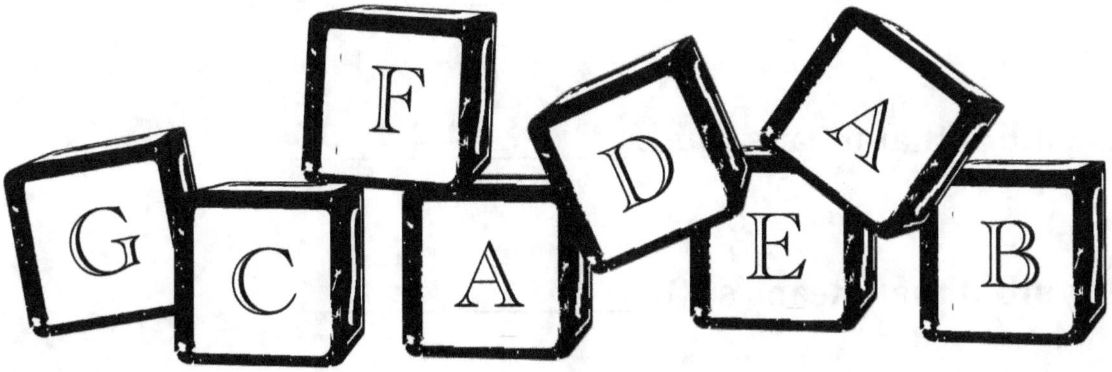

3. Fill in the missing letters of the music alphabet.

4. Write the letters in the blocks that come before and after the letter in the middle block.

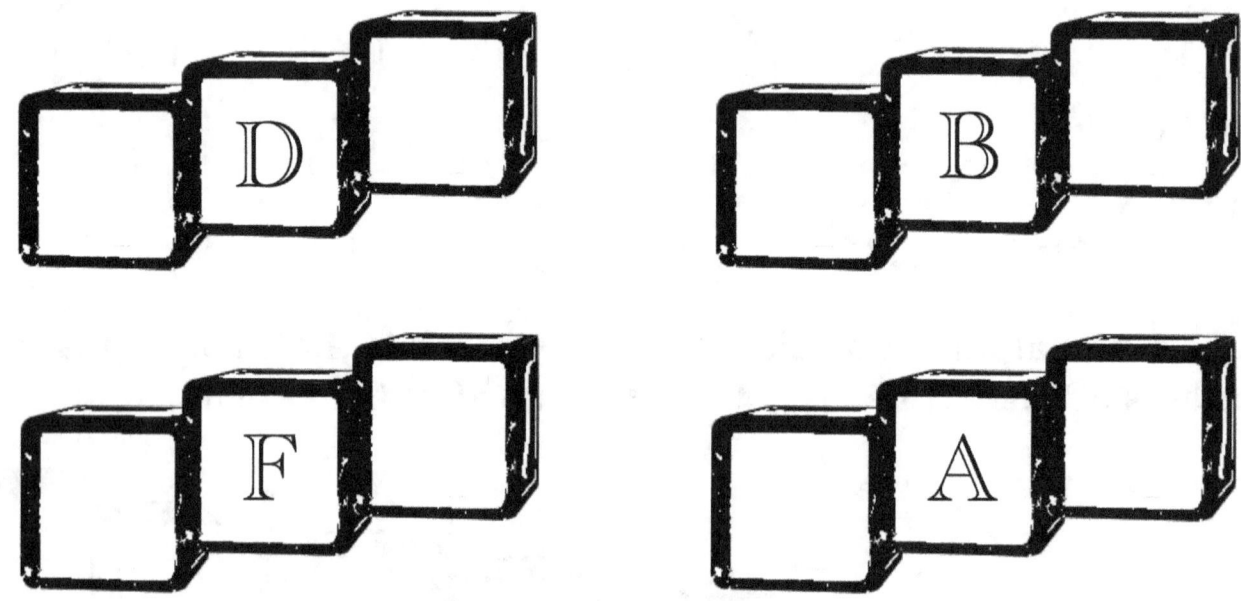

5. The lowest sounding cello string is _____.

6. The highest sounding cello string is _____.

7. Draw the symbol that means loud. _____

8. Draw the symbol that means soft. _____

34

Finger Number Bingo

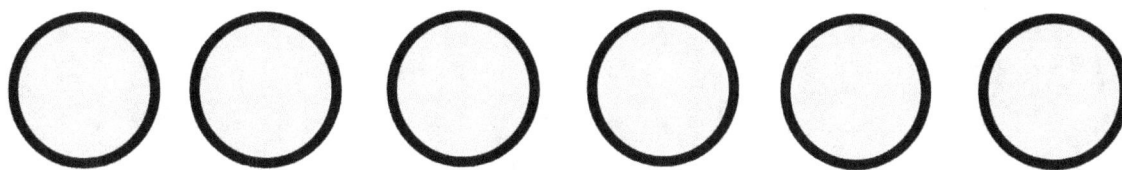

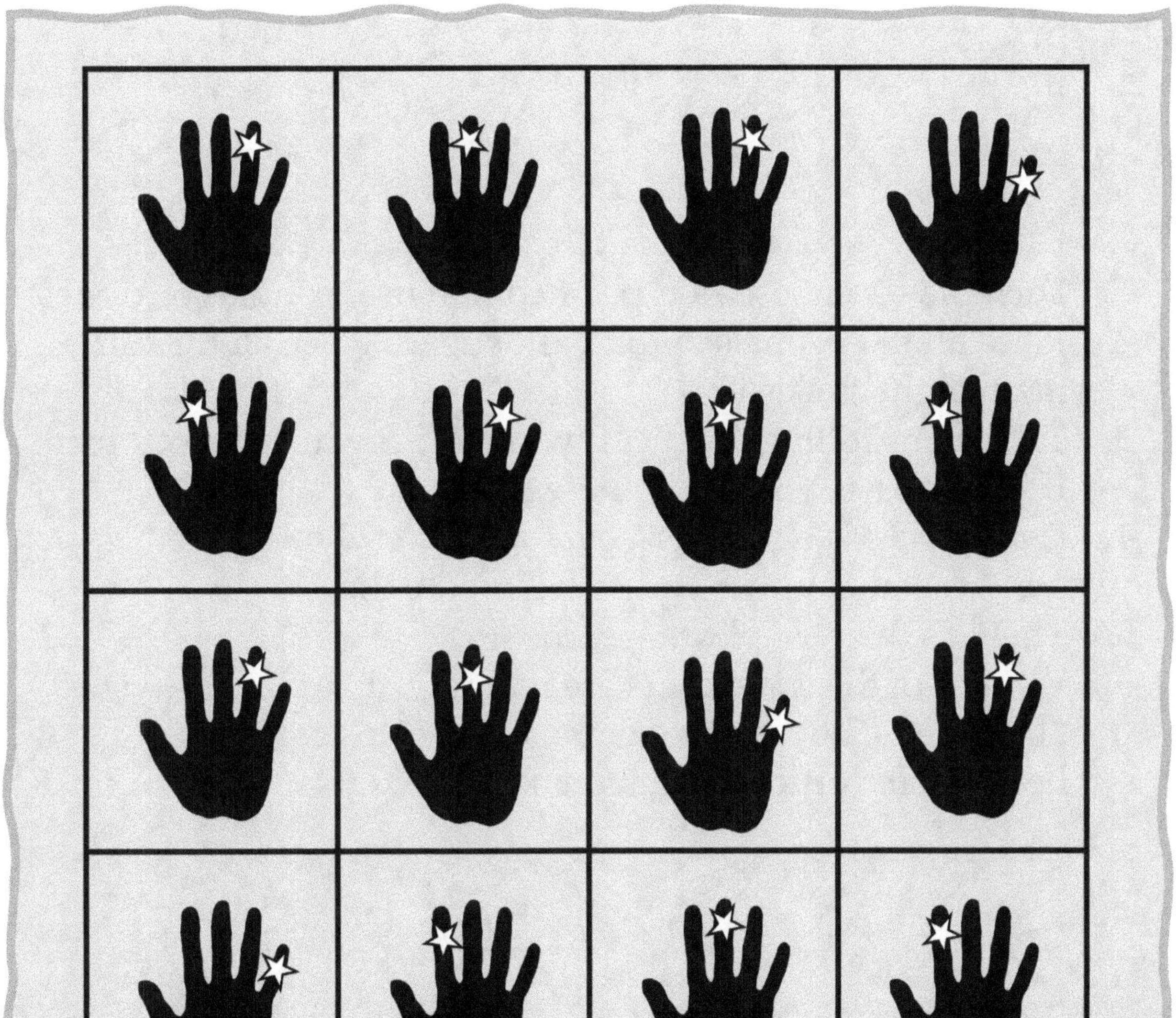

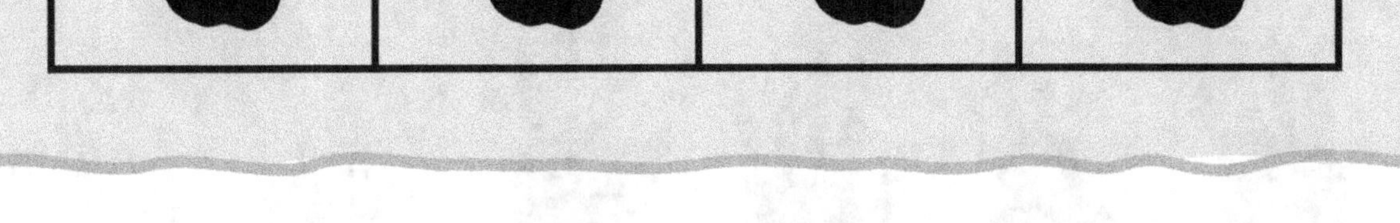

Finger Number Bingo

2 Players

What you need:
    6 pennies
    6 dimes
    1 die

How to play:

1. Each player chooses a type of coin to use, pennies or dimes.
2. Place all the pennies in the dark circles. Place all the dimes in the light circles.
3. Take turns rolling the die. If you roll a 5 you lose your turn. If you roll a 6, you can roll the die again.
4. Using one of your coins, cover any box whose finger matches the number you rolled on the die.
5. Then it's the next player's turn.
6. When 4 of the same coins are in a row, that player says "BINGO!" They are the winner! The coins can be horizontal, vertical or diagonal.

Lesson 13

Each finger on the left hand has a house on the A string. Each thin line on the fingerboard is where the finger lives. Your teacher put tapes on your cello to show where the houses are on your fingerboard. The letters go up in the music alphabet as you put fingers on the A string.

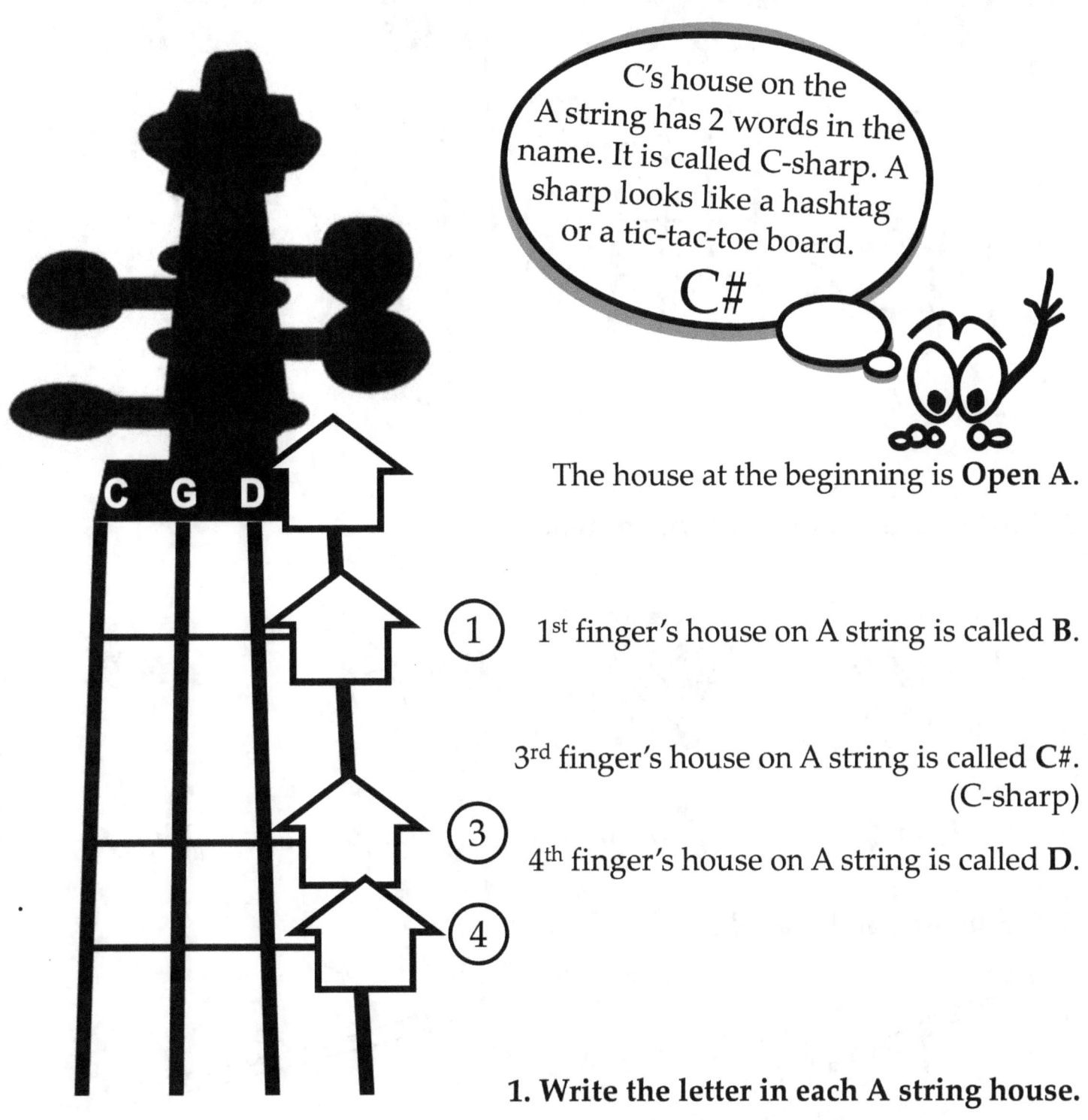

C's house on the A string has 2 words in the name. It is called C-sharp. A sharp looks like a hashtag or a tic-tac-toe board.
C#

The house at the beginning is **Open A.**

① 1st finger's house on A string is called **B.**

3rd finger's house on A string is called **C#.** (C-sharp)

③

④ 4th finger's house on A string is called **D.**

1. Write the letter in each A string house.

2. Write the letter in each A string house.

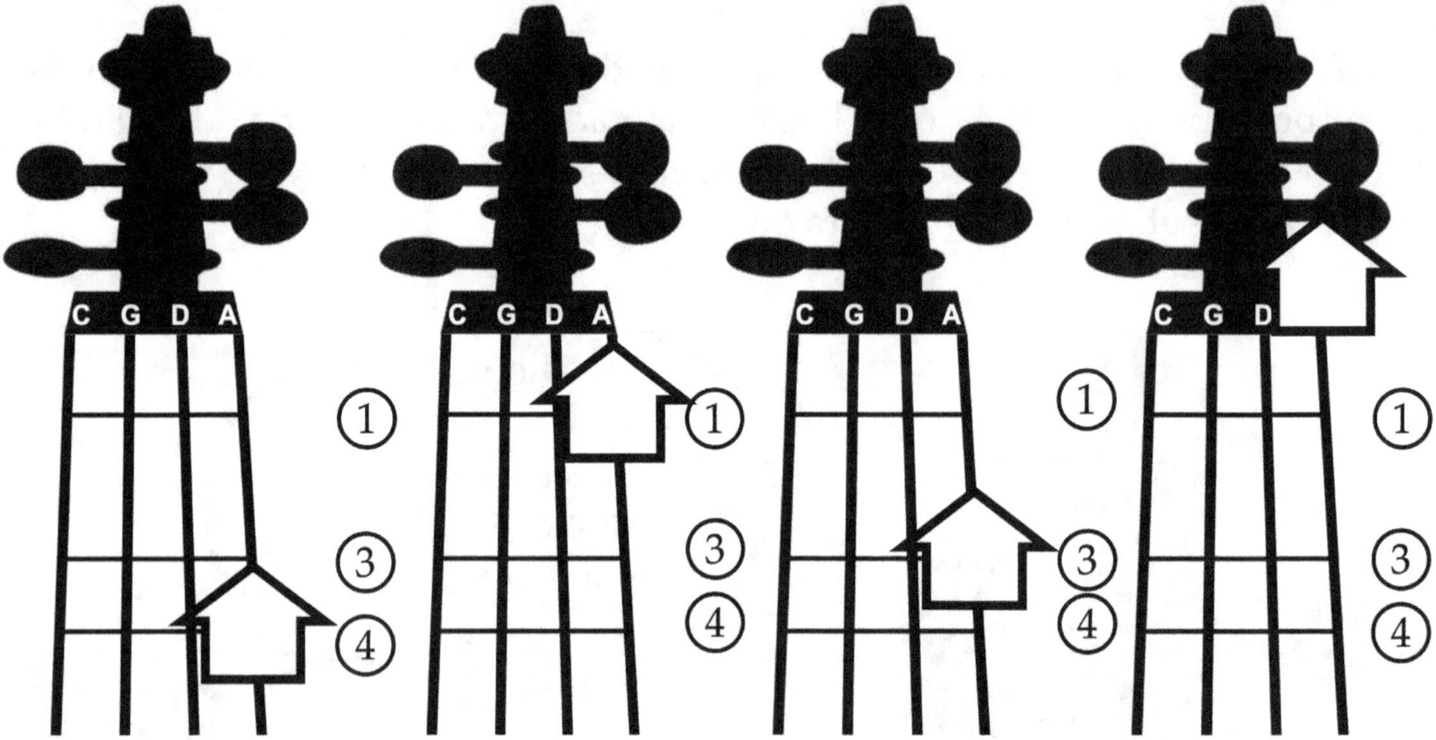

C G D A   ① ③ ④

C G D A   ① ③ ④

C G D A   ① ③ ④

C G D   ① ③ ④

3. Circle the dynamic for each animal.

f or *p*   *f* or *p*   *f* or *p*   *f* or *p*

4. Circle the hand that plays.

Right Hand   **Left Hand**   **Right Hand**   **Left Hand**

Lesson 14

1. Write the music alphabet in order in the blocks.

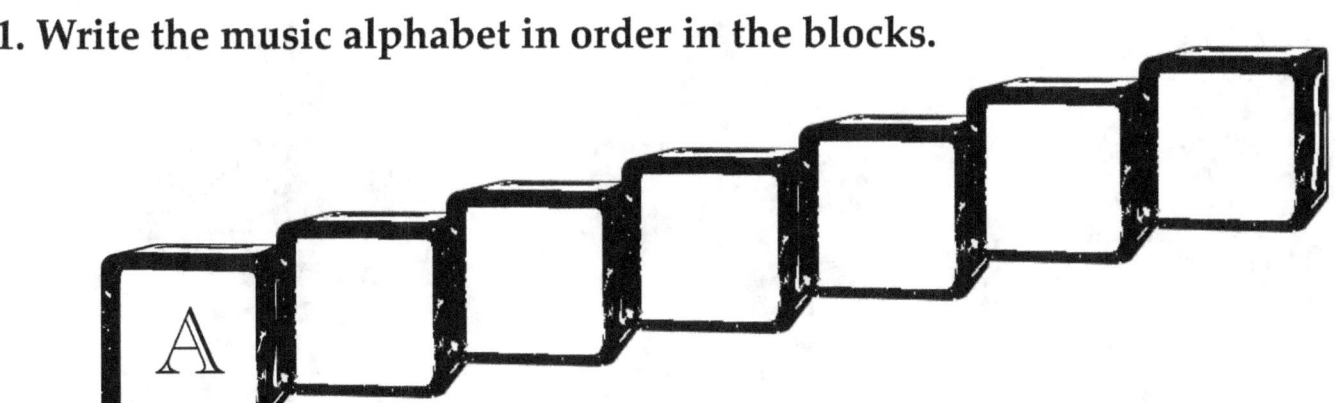

2. Sing the music alphabet song. Sing the regular English alphabet song, but instead of singing "H, I, J, K…" start over at A. Keep repeating the music alphabet until you get to the end of the song!

Did you know that we can say the music alphabet starting on any letter? Begin on any letter and remember the letter A comes after G! Stop on the same letter that you started with.

3. Point to each letter and say the music alphabet starting and ending on B.

4. Point to each letter and say the music alphabet starting and ending on D.

5. Write the finger number in the circle that plays the note on the A string.

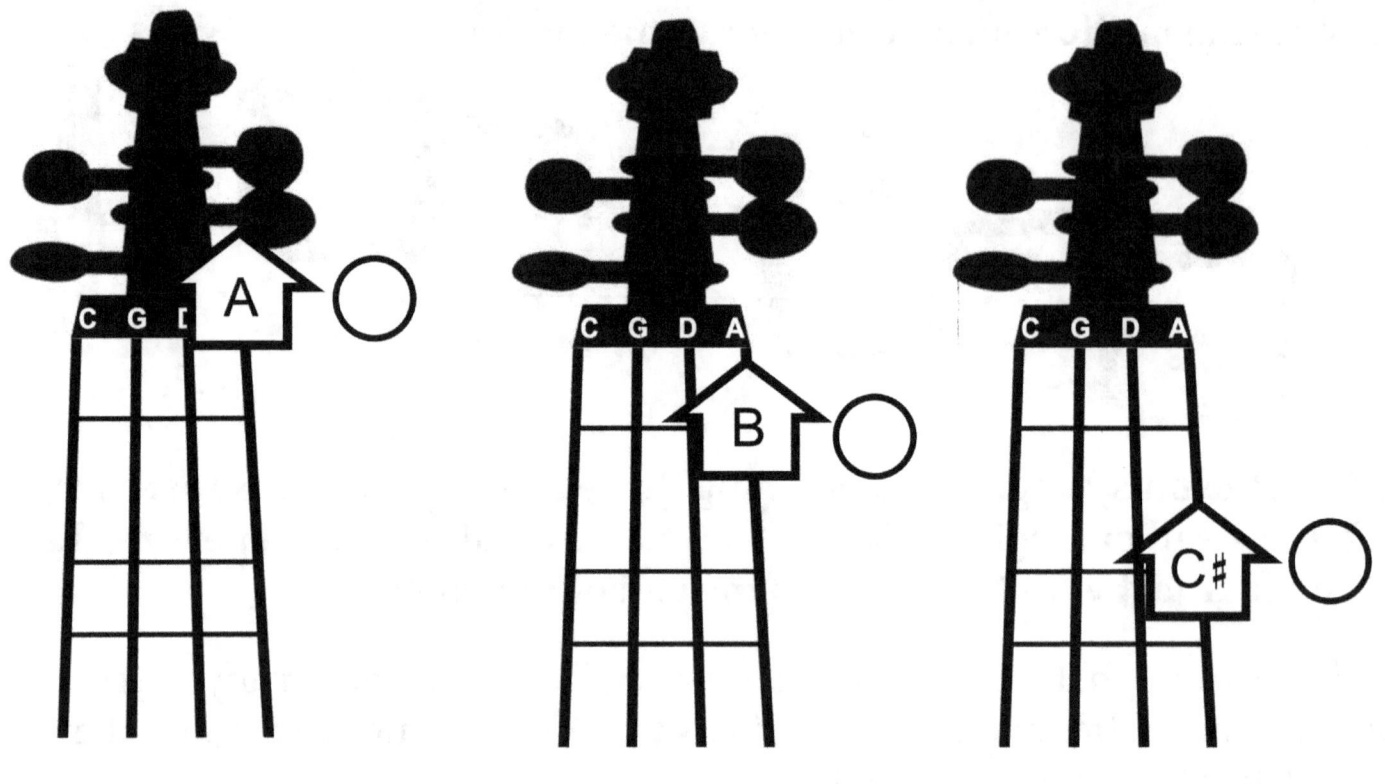

6. Listen as your teacher plays the notes on the A string, starting on A. Did you hear the notes get higher? They are going up!

7. Listen as your teacher plays the notes on the A string starting with 4th finger D going backwards The notes get lower. They are going down.

Lesson 15

Each finger on the left hand has a house on the D string. The house letters are different on the D string than on the A string. The houses on the D string go up through the music alphabet starting on D.

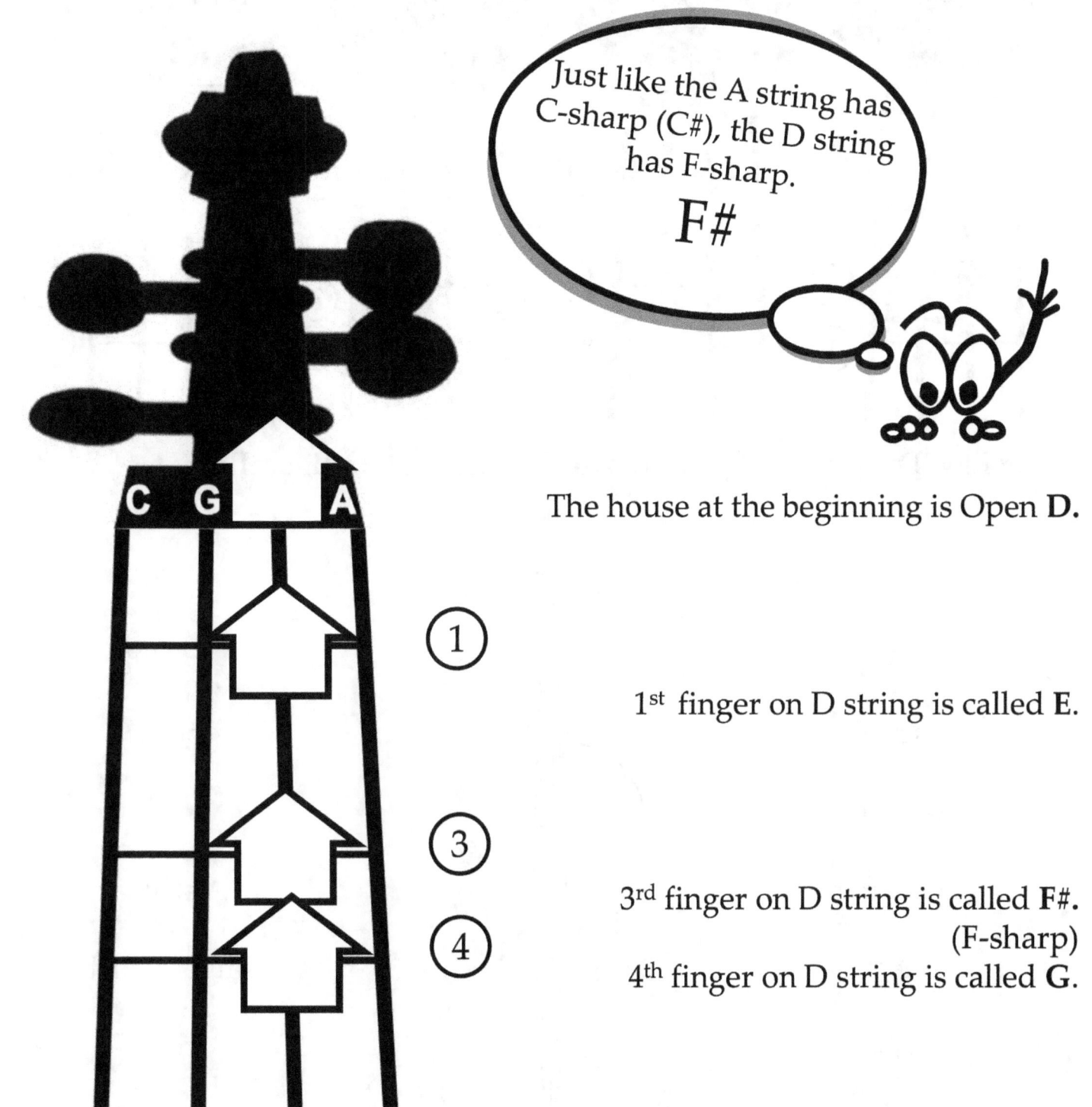

Just like the A string has C-sharp (C#), the D string has F-sharp.

F#

The house at the beginning is Open **D.**

1st finger on D string is called **E.**

3rd finger on D string is called **F#.** (F-sharp)

4th finger on D string is called **G.**

1. Write the letter in each D string house.

2. Write the correct letter in each D string house.

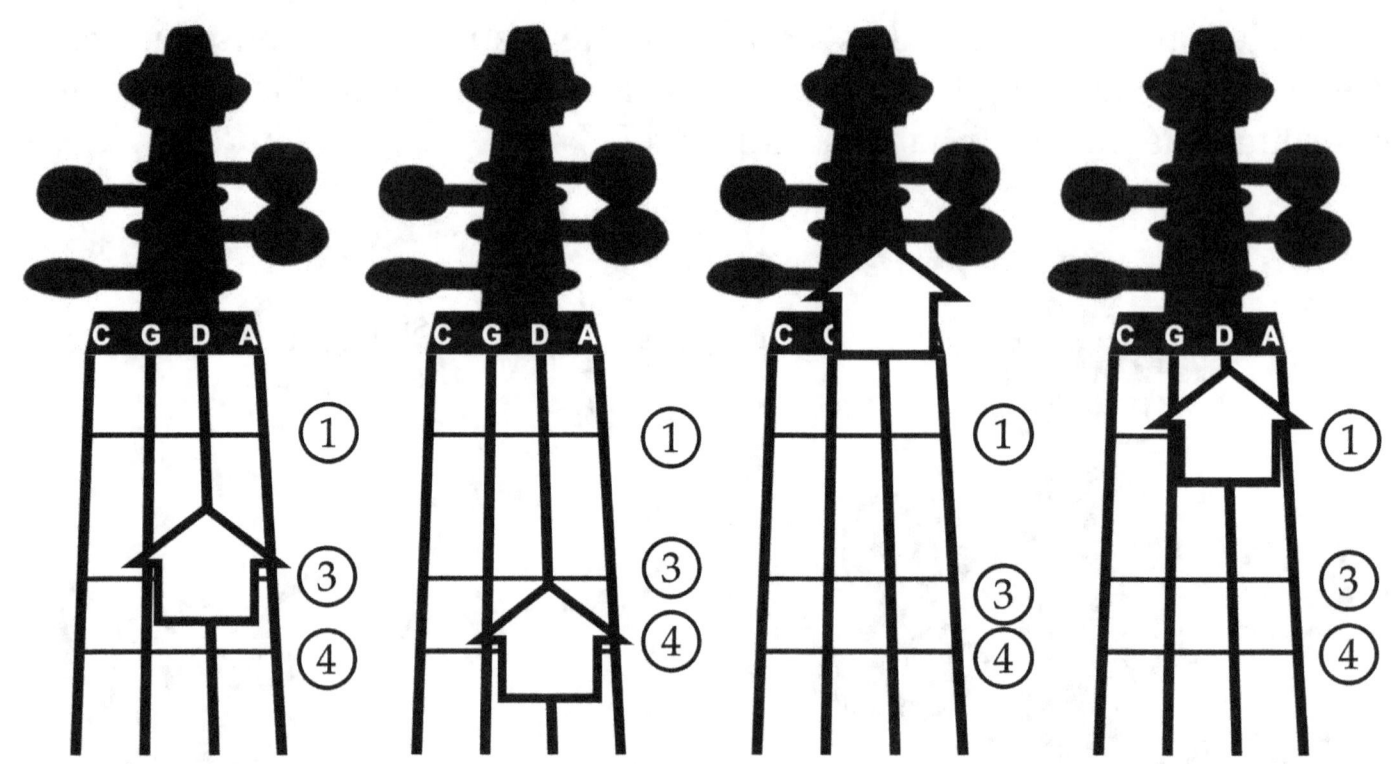

3. Review: Draw a line from the word to the part on the cello.

endpin

scroll

G string

C string

neck

ribs

bridge

fine tuners

D string

pegs

nut

A string

fingerboard

front

F holes

tailpiece

Lesson 16

1. **Fill in all the house letters on the D string and on the A string. Don't forget to write a sharp by the letters F# and C#.**

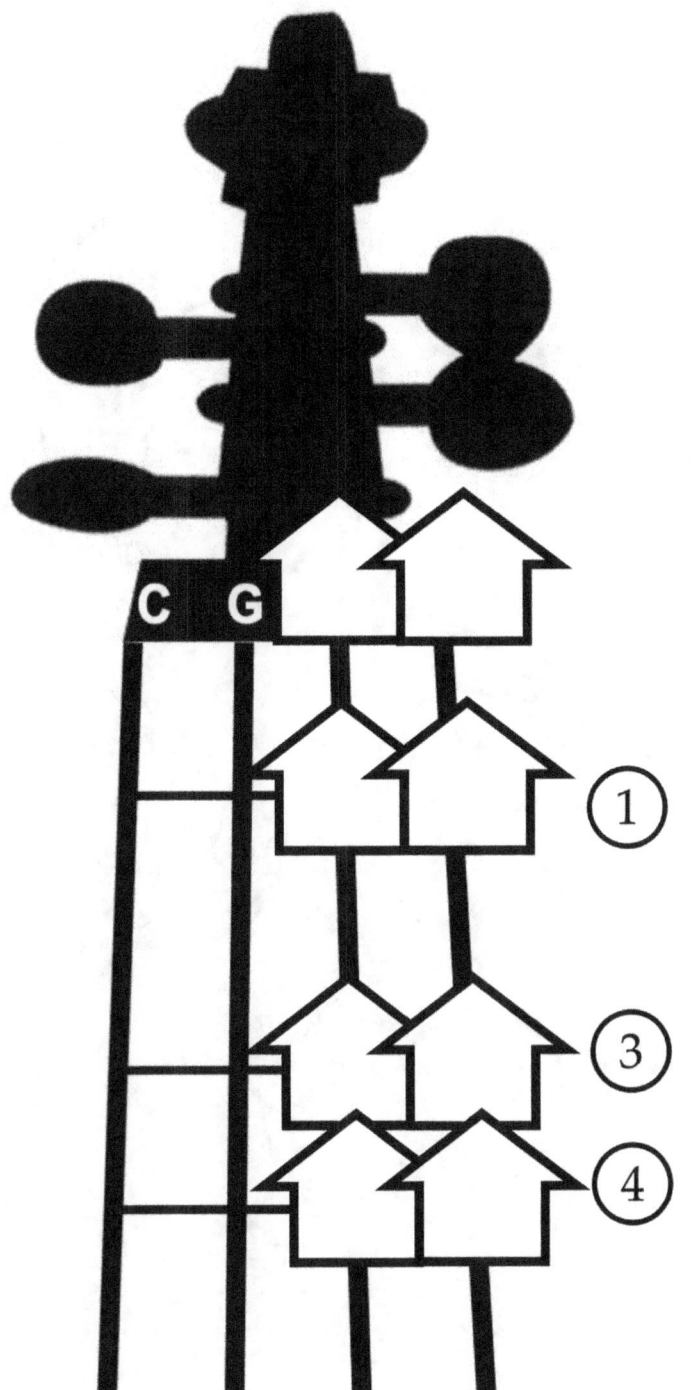

Two houses on the are getting packages today. House D and house A have packages. Help the driver find the distance between D & A.

2. **Begin counting with A and count the number of houses between D and A. Write the number on the line.**

_____

What do you hear? #4

Help Sally Squirrel know if it is a D or an A acorn. Circle the name of the string you hear.

1 D A

2 D A

3 D A

4 D A

5 D A

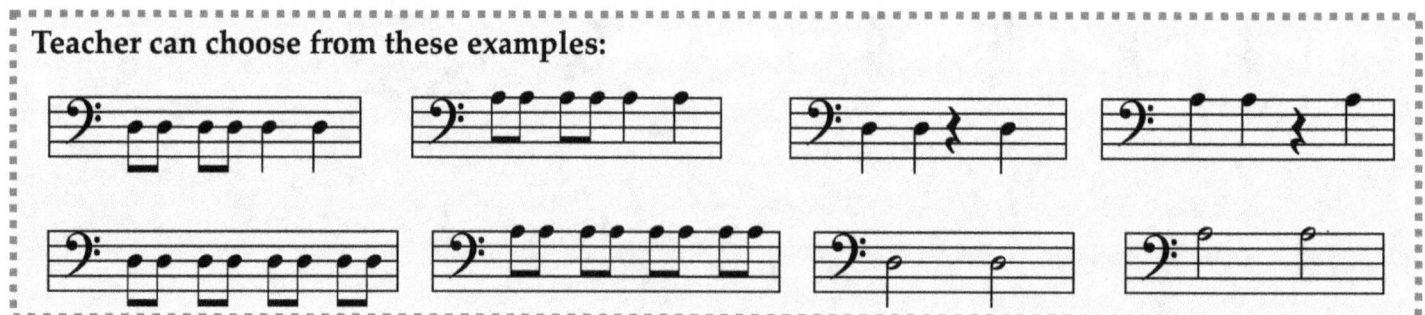

Teacher can choose from these examples:

The Magic of Music Theory Pre-Reading A - © 2024 Horsehair Music. Photocopying prohibited.

Lesson 17

You have a beat inside you. It is your heartbeat! Can you feel the beat in you? Music has a beat like your beat. We use notes to show beats in music. This is a **quarter note**, and it gets 1 beat. The quarter note has 2 parts, the **note head** and the **stem**. The stem can go up or down!

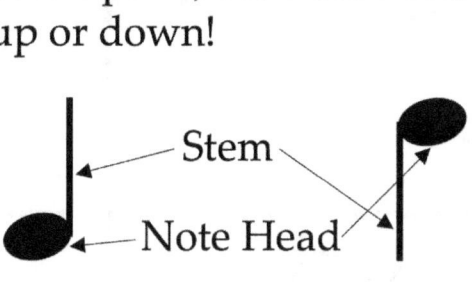

An up stem is always on the right side of the note head.

1. Trace the notes and color in the note head to make them quarter notes.

A down stem is *always* on the left side of the note head.

2. Trace the notes with down stems and color in the note head to make them quarter notes.

To draw a quarter note, draw a circle. Color it in. Then, draw a stem going up on the right side, or down on the left side.

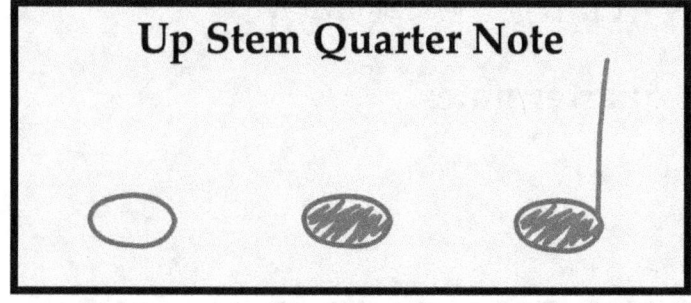

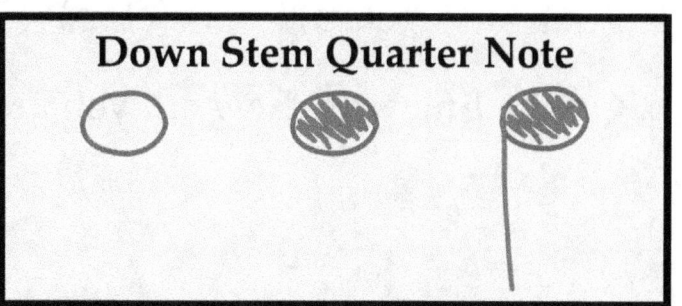

3. Draw a quarter note in each box. Then, in the heart write a 1 for the quarter note beat. You may choose an up or down stem. (Remember stems go up on the right, down on the left.)

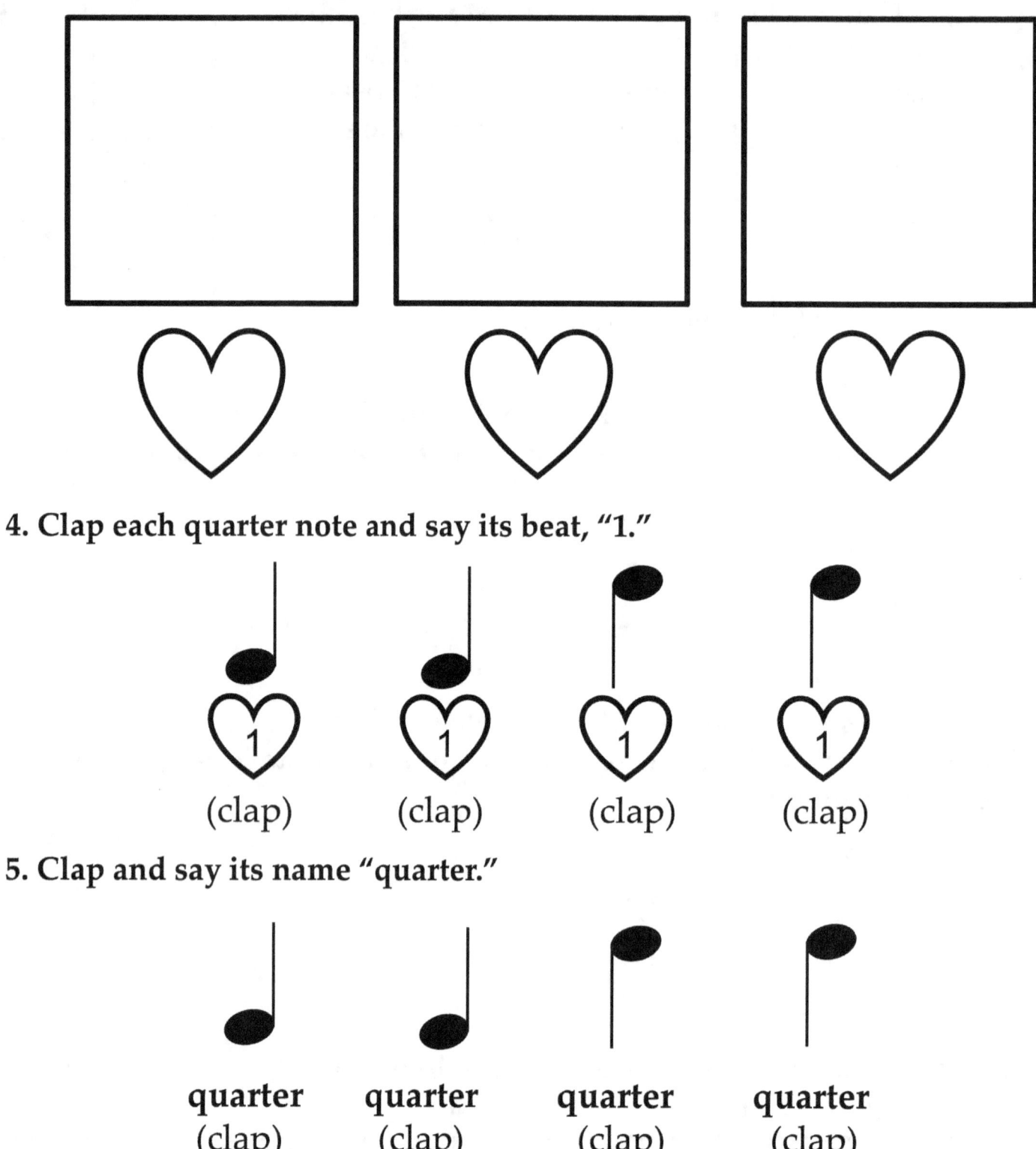

4. Clap each quarter note and say its beat, "1."

(clap)   (clap)   (clap)   (clap)

5. Clap and say its name "quarter."

quarter   quarter   quarter   quarter
(clap)   (clap)   (clap)   (clap)

6. On the line write how old you are in quarter notes.

Lesson 18

This is a **half note**. The half note looks like the quarter note, except the note head is *not* colored in! Half notes have 2 beats inside them.

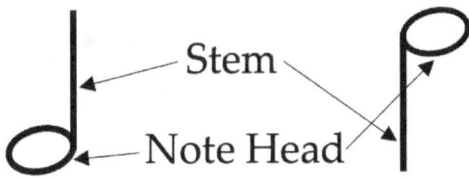

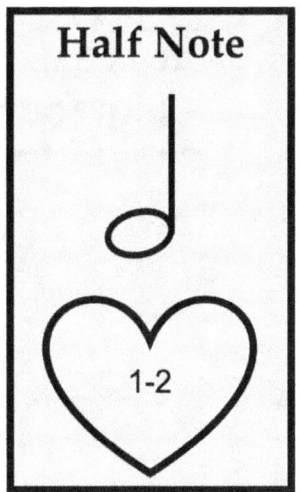

Half Note

1. Trace the dots or each half note. But don't color them in!

2. Clap each half note and say its beats. To clap a half note, clap and say "1." Then hold your hands together while you say "2."

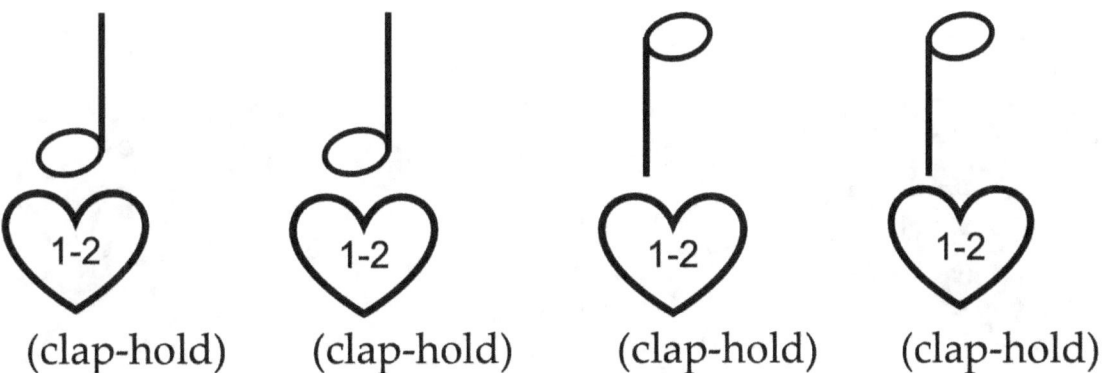

1-2	1-2	1-2	1-2
(clap-hold)	(clap-hold)	(clap-hold)	(clap-hold)

3. Clap each half note and say its name. Clap 1 time when you say "half." Then hold your hands together while you say "note."

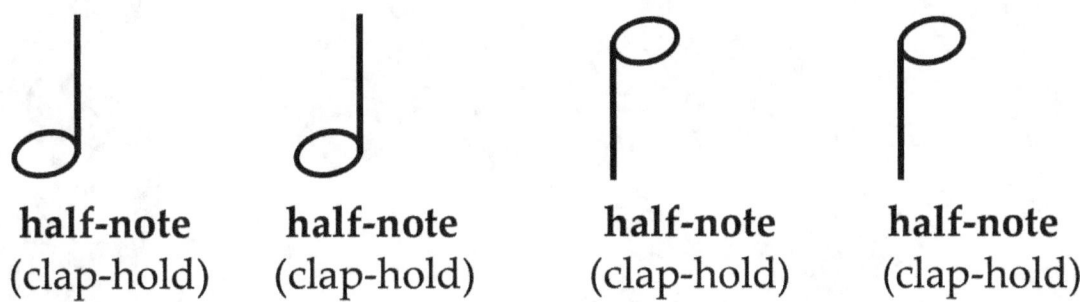

half-note	**half-note**	**half-note**	**half-note**
(clap-hold)	(clap-hold)	(clap-hold)	(clap-hold)

Draw half notes just like quarter notes, but don't color in the note head!

4. Draw a half note in each box. Then in the heart underneath write a 1-2 for the half note beats. You may choose an up or down stem.

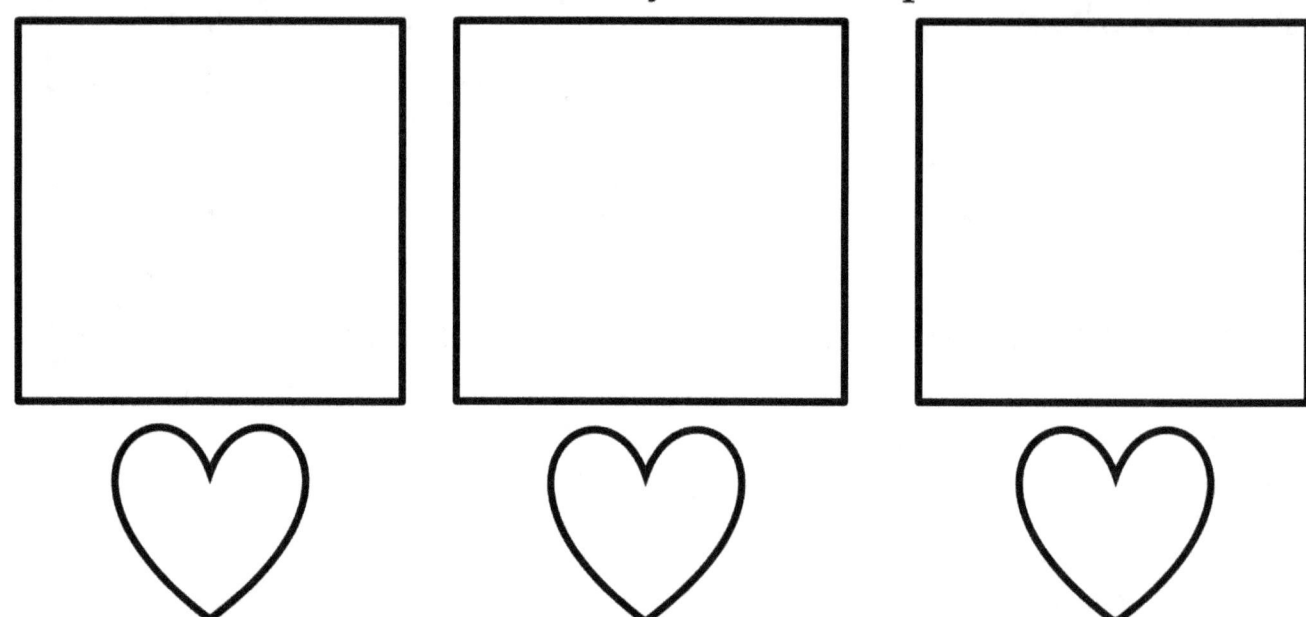

5. These aliens want to make it back to Planet Quarter Note and Planet Half Note! Draw a line matching each alien's note tattoo to the correct spaceship.

Lesson 19

We read the notes from left to right just like we read words in a book. As the notes get higher on the page, the sound will go up. As the notes move lower on the page, the sound will go down. If the notes do not go up or down but are in a straight line, they will sound the same.

1. Trace the line from one note head to the next note head.

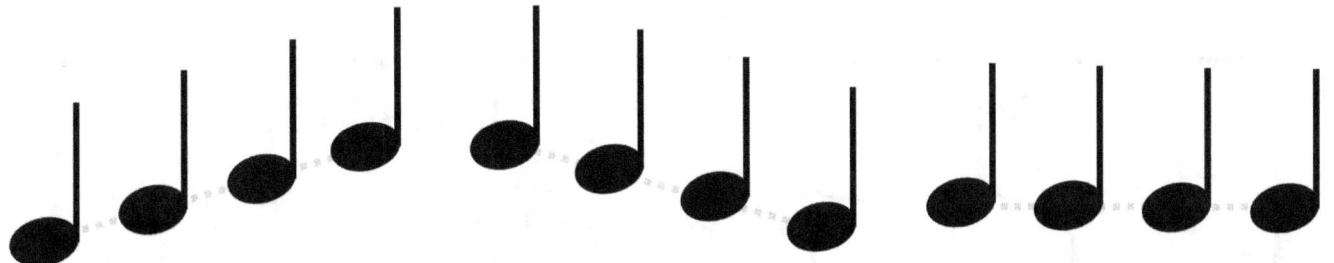

The notes go UP   The notes go DOWN   These stay the SAME

2. Draw a line connecting the note heads. Circle if the notes go up, down, or stay the same.

A.

UP   DOWN   SAME

B.

UP   DOWN   SAME

C.

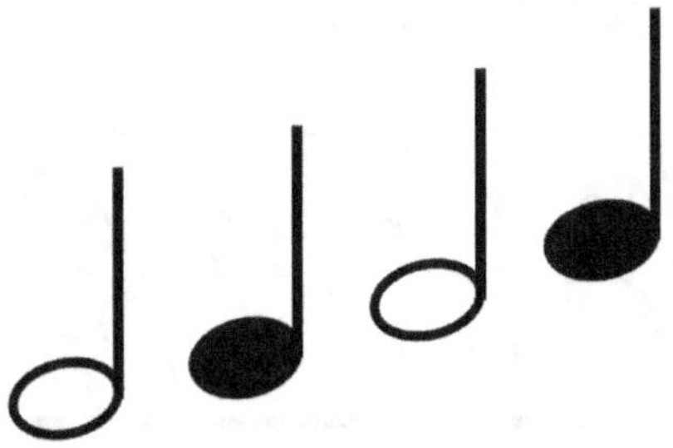

UP   DOWN   SAME

D.

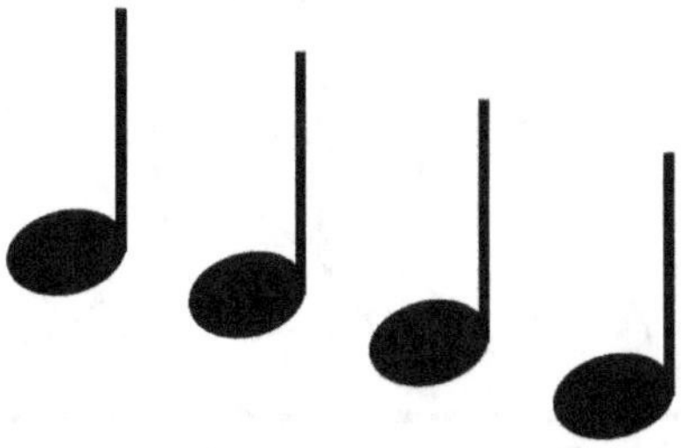

UP   DOWN   SAME

E.

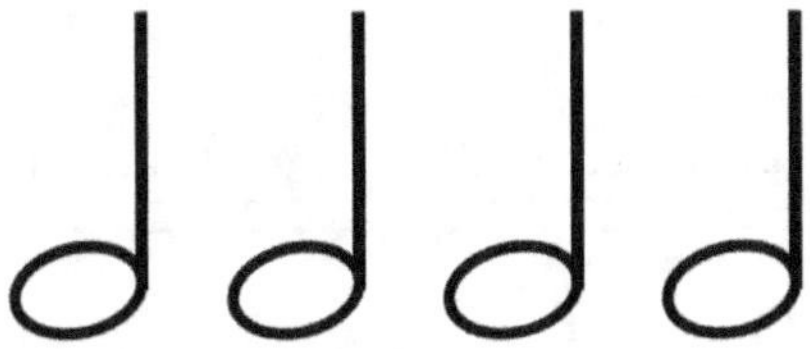

UP   DOWN   SAME

F.

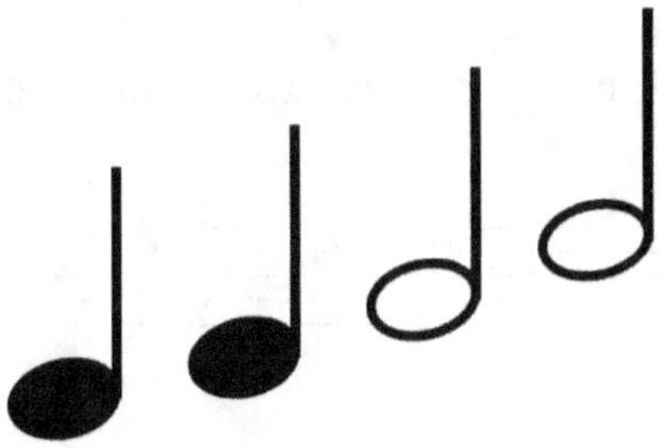

UP   DOWN   SAME

What do you hear? #5

You will hear 3 notes. If you hear the same note 3 times, color the leaves that are the same. If you hear 3 notes that are different, color the leaves that are different.

1.

SAME   DIFFERENT

2.

SAME   DIFFERENT

3.

SAME   DIFFERENT

The teacher may choose from these examples:

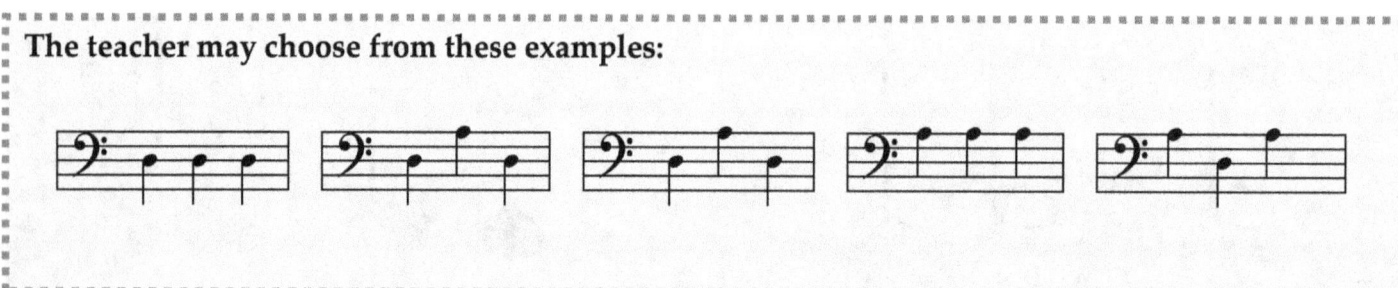

Lesson 20

1. Write the beats for each note in the hearts. Then, circle if the notes are moving up, down or staying the same.

UP   DOWN   SAME   UP   DOWN   SAME

2. Clap and say their names.

3. Write the letter name in each house.

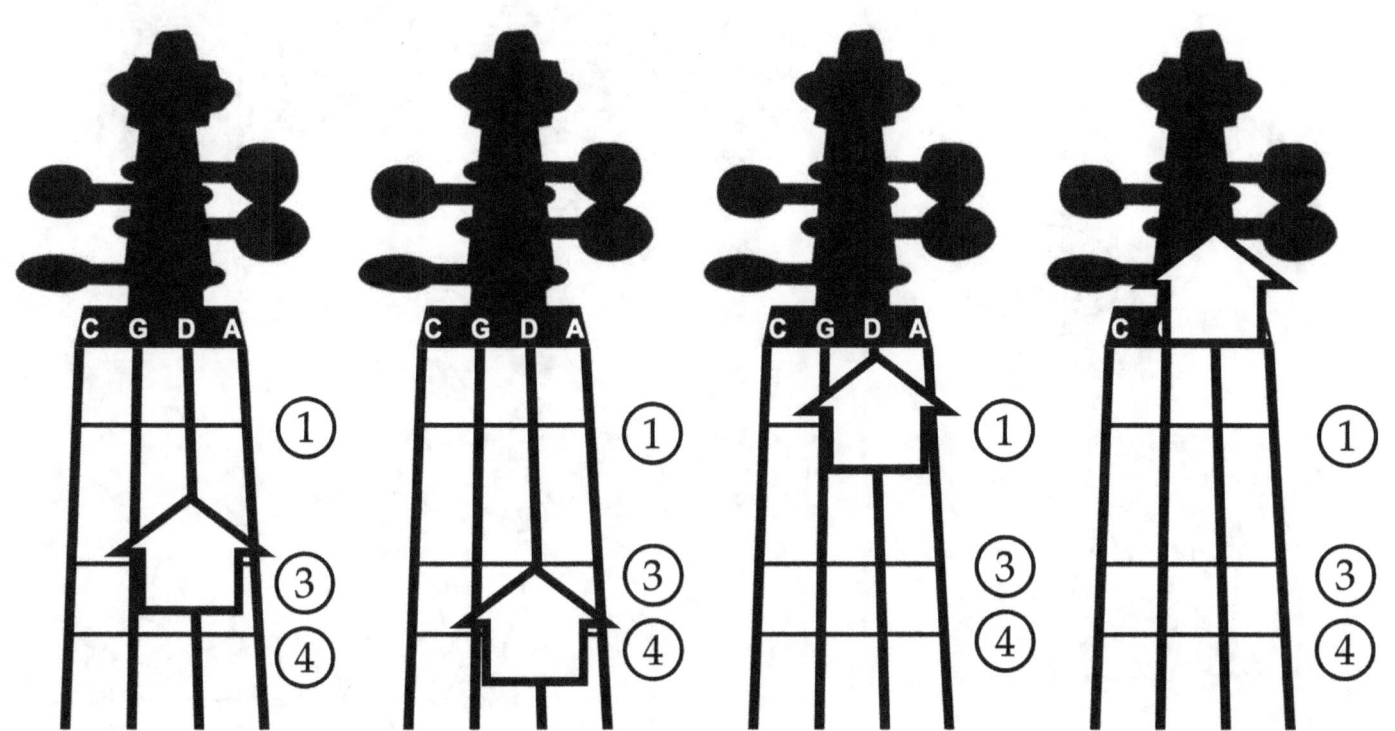

4. Farmer McDonald needs to get his pigs to the correct barn. Draw a line from the note on the pig to the barn where it lives.

Lesson 21

1. Write the missing letters in each house on the fingerboard.

Write the finger number for each question.

What finger plays D? _____
(on the D string)

What finger plays E? _____
(on the D string)

What finger plays F#? _____

What finger plays G? _____

What finger plays A? _____
(on the A string)

What finger plays B? _____

What finger plays C#? _____

What finger plays D? _____
(on the A string)

3. Can you find the hidden notes? Circle the quarter notes. Draw a square around the half note.

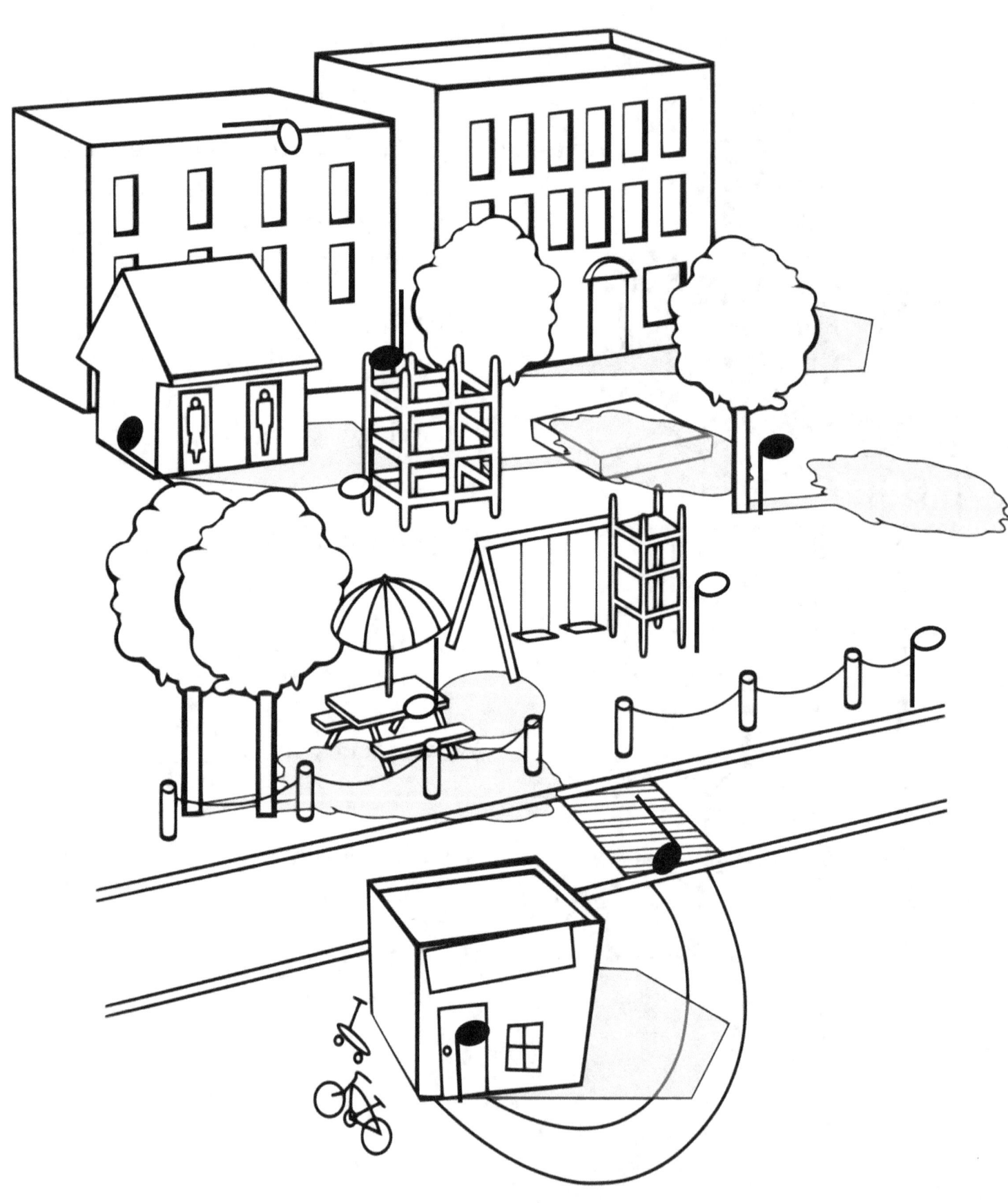

Lesson 22

This is a **dotted half note**. It is a half note with a dot! A dotted half notes have 3 beats inside them.

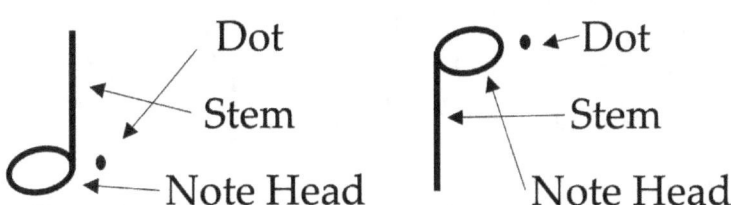

Dotted Half Note

1. Trace the dotted lines to draw a dotted half note. Color the dots.

2. Clap each dotted half note and say its beats. To clap a dotted half note, clap and say "1." Then hold your hands together while you say "2-3."

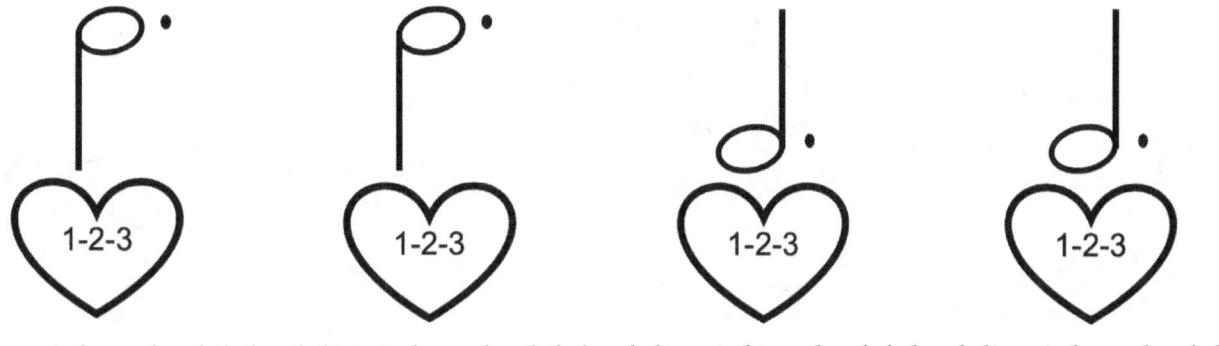

(clap-hold-hold)   (clap-hold-hold)   (clap-hold-hold)   (clap-hold-hold)

3. Clap each dotted half note and say its name. Clap 1 time when you say "half." Then hold your hands together while you say "note-dot."

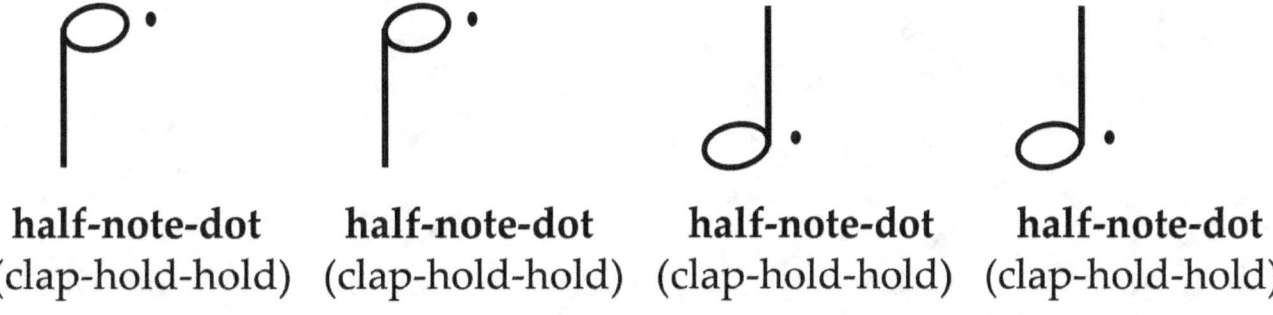

half-note-dot   **half-note-dot**   **half-note-dot**   **half-note-dot**
(clap-hold-hold)   (clap-hold-hold)   (clap-hold-hold)   (clap-hold-hold)

55

3. Write the number of beats for each note in the hearts.

4. Draw a note in the hat that equals the number of beats in the heart.

3

1

2

1

3

5. Clap the notes and say their beats. Then clap and say their names.

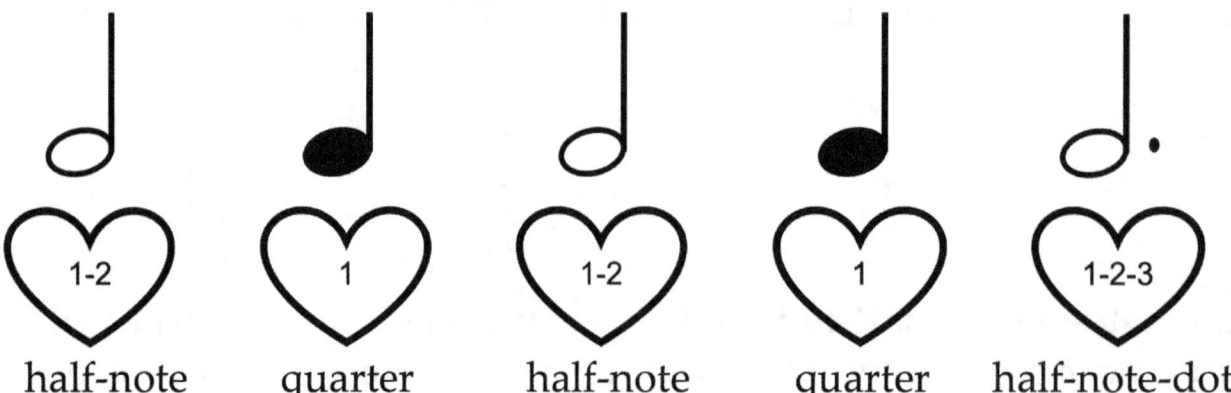

1-2	1	1-2	1	1-2-3
half-note	quarter	half-note	quarter	half-note-dot

Lesson 23

This is a **whole note**. Whole notes have 4 beats inside them. It is just a round oval. There is only a note head. There is no stem!

 ←——Note Head

1. Trace the dotted lines to draw whole notes.

2. Clap each whole note and say its beats. Clap and say "1." Then hold your hands together while you say "2-3-4."

(clap-hold-hold-hold)   (clap-hold-hold-hold)   (clap-hold-hold-hold)

3. Clap each whole note and say its name. Clap and say "whole." Then hold your hands together while you say "note-4-beats."

whole-note-4-beats   **whole-note-4-beats**   **whole-note-4-beats**
(clap-hold-hold-hold)   (clap-hold-hold-hold)   (clap-hold-hold-hold)

4. Write the beats in the heart under each note.

5. Let's go snorkeling! Snorkel your way through and circle if the notes move up, down, or stay the same.

Lesson 24

1. Say the name of the insect and clap each syllable. Write the number of claps in each heart. Then draw the note in the box that equals the number of beats.

Bee

Dra-gon-fly

Spi-der

Bee-tle

Ant

Cat-er-pil-lar

What do you hear? #6

Color the dolphin if you hear your teacher play the D string. Color the ant if you hear the A string. Then, circle whether you hear forte or piano.

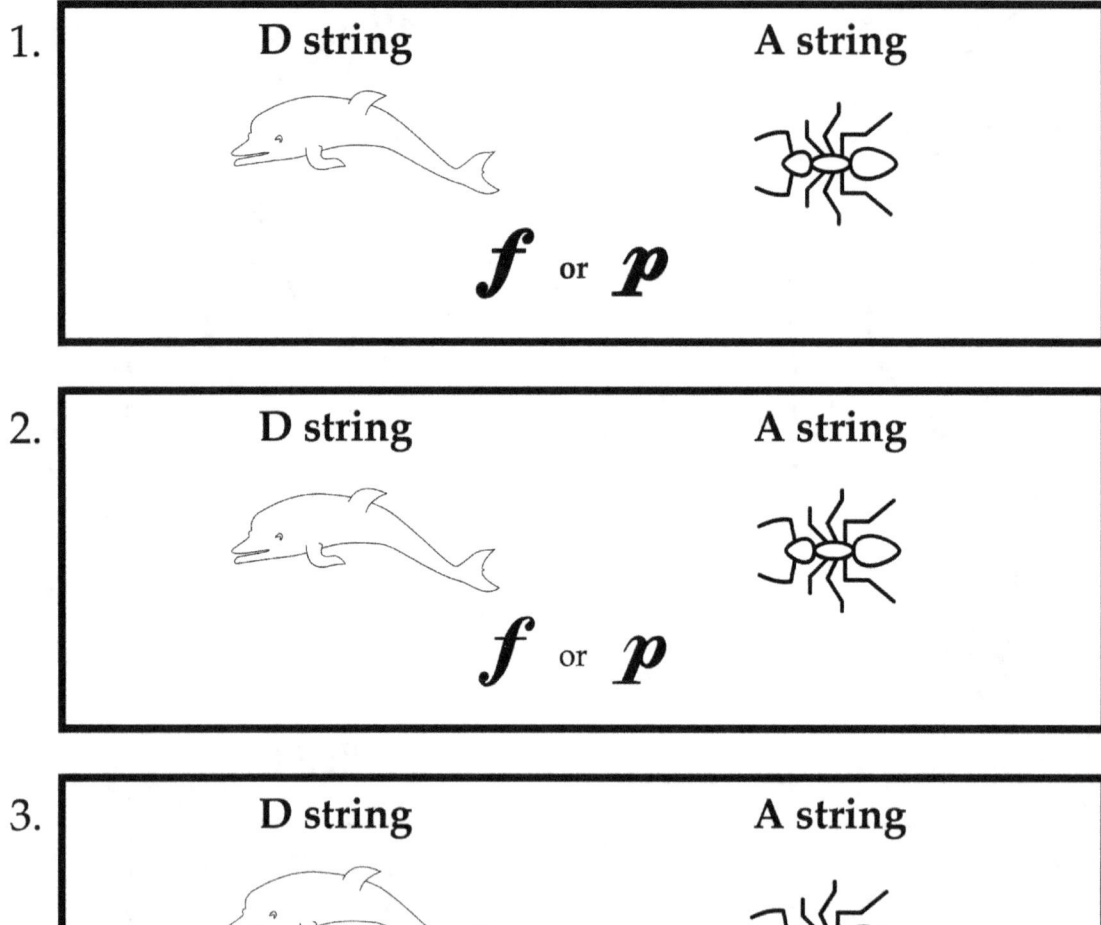

1. D string   A string

f or p

2. D string   A string

f or p

3. D string   A string

f or p

Teacher can choose from these examples and choose the dynamic to play:

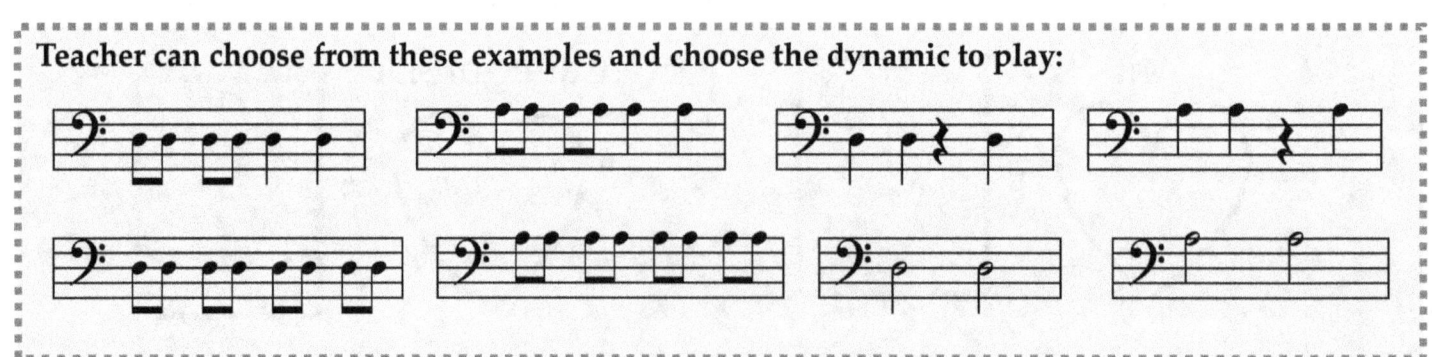

Lesson 25

There are some unusual pets living in the fingerboard houses. Draw a line matching the first letter of the animal's name to the house with the same letter.

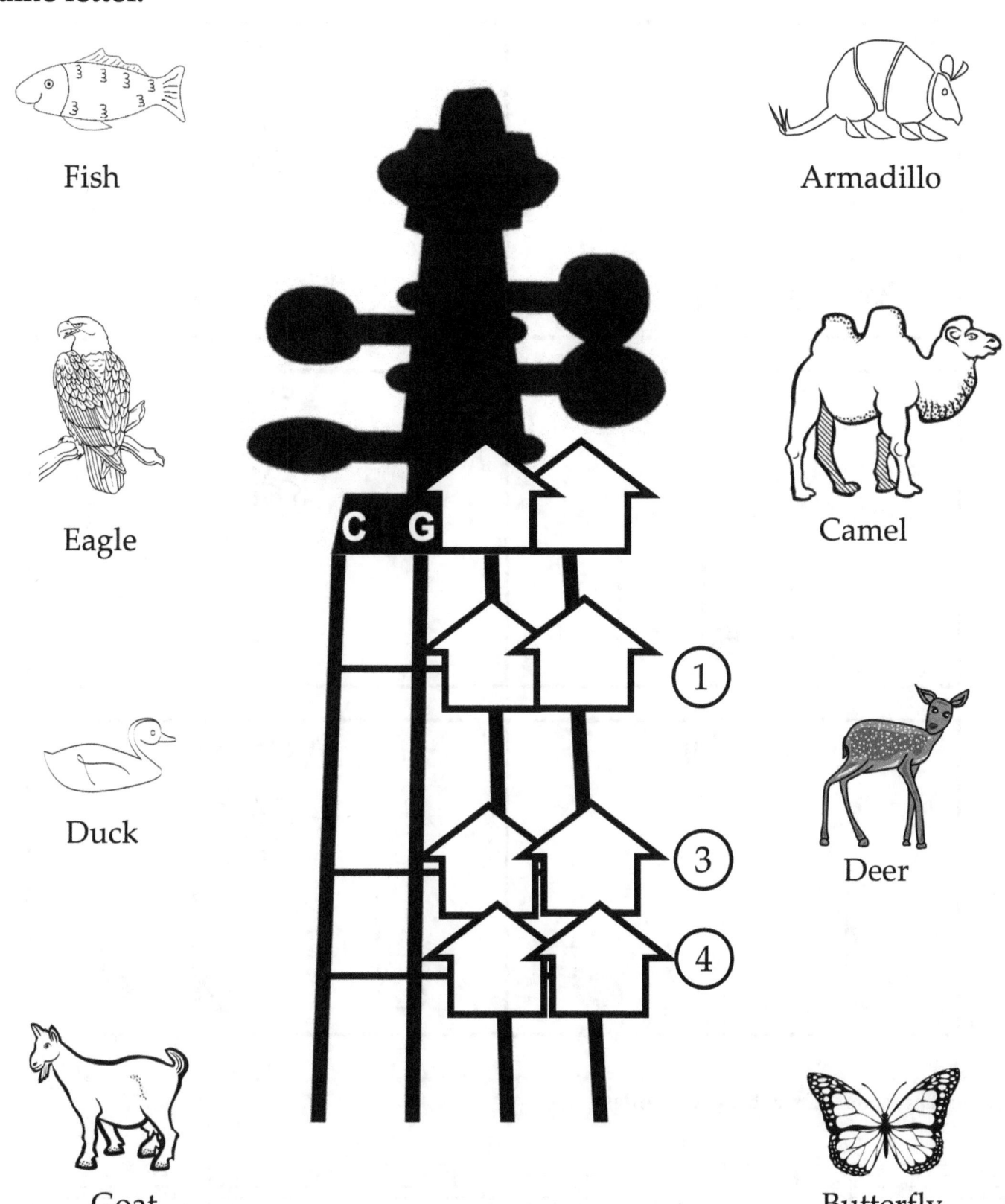

Fish

Armadillo

Eagle

Camel

Duck

Deer

Goat

Butterfly

What do you hear? #7

Circle the box that you hear.

1.
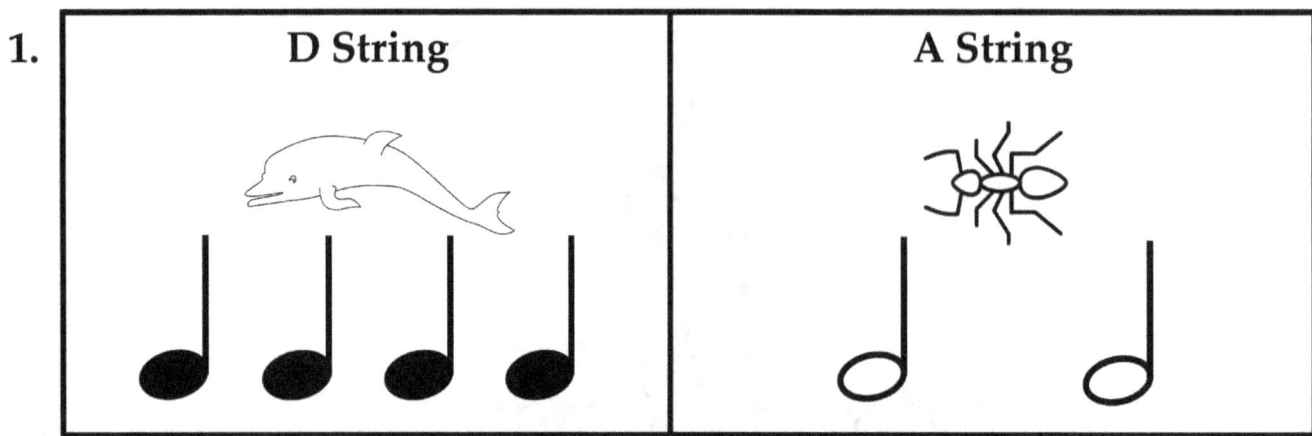

2.
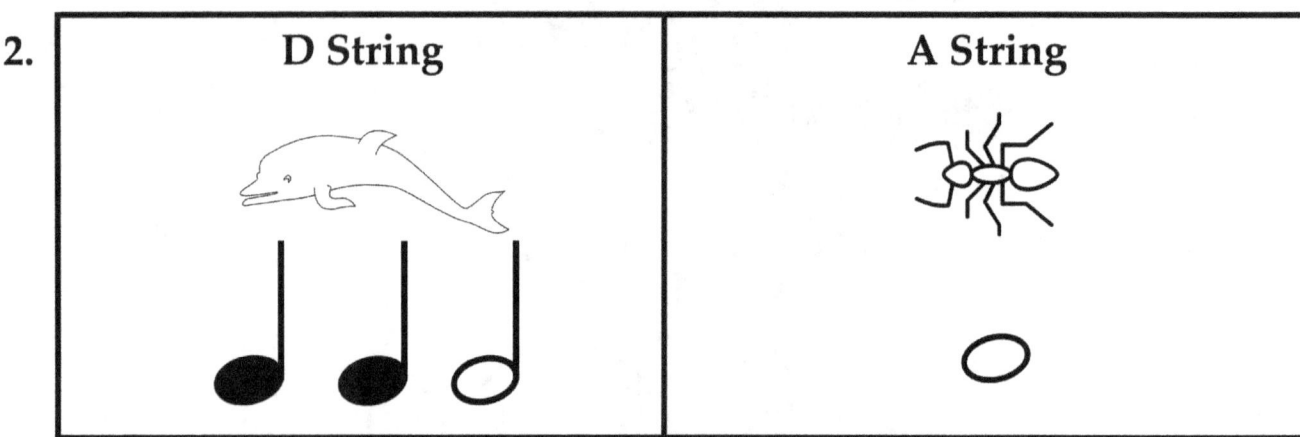

3.
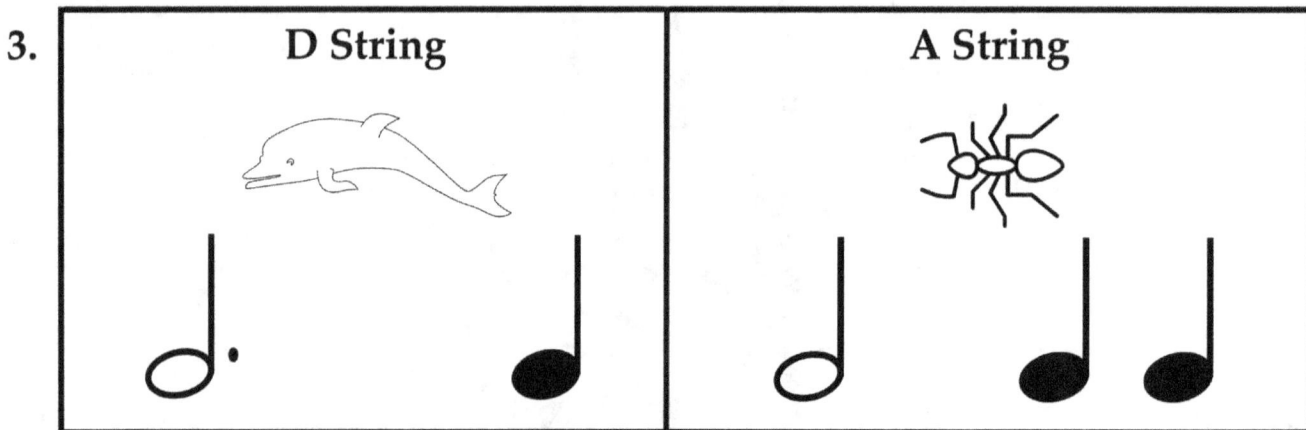

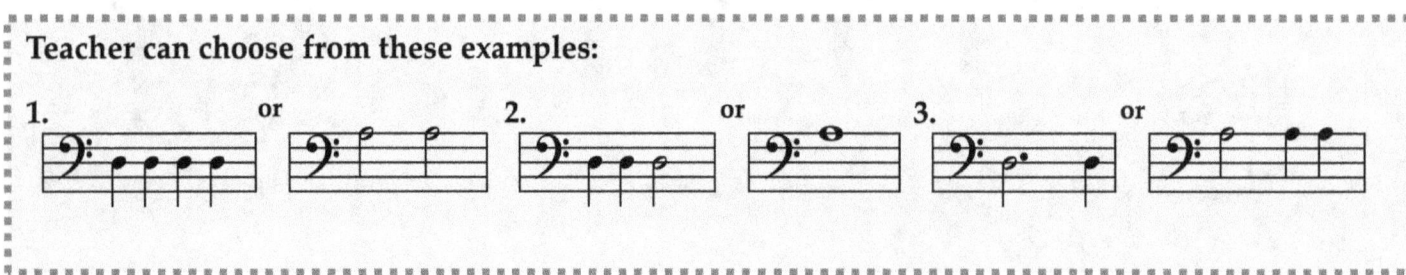
62

A & D Apple Orchard

2 Players

What you need:
- 5 pennies
- 5 dimes
- 1 die
- 2 cups

How to play:

1. Each player chooses the type of coin they wants to use, pennies or dimes.
2. Place your coins in a pile or cup near the game board.
3. Take turns rolling the die. The number that you roll on the die equals a finger number. Place one of your coins on an apple letter that is played by that finger number on the fingerboard.
4. The first player to place all his coins on the tree wins.
5. If you roll and there is no letter that matches that finger, the next player takes a turn.

E or B	Roll Again	F# or C#	G or D	xxxx	Wild!
				Loose A Turn	Choose any and say the finger number

REVIEW

1. Write the letters for each open string in the house.

2. Draw a quarter note in the box.

3. Draw a half note in the box.

4. Draw a dotted half note in the box.

5. Draw a whole note in the box.

6. Circle the symbol that means loud!

f p

7. Circle the symbol that means soft!

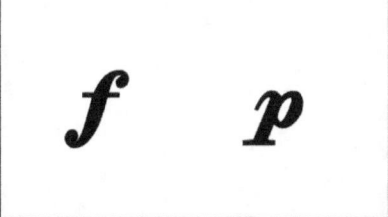

65

Glossary

A String – Highest string on the cello.

D String – Second string from the left on the cello.

Dotted Half Note – Gets 3 beats in 4/4 time.

Forte – [dynamic] Italian word meaning loud.

Half Note – Gets 2 beats in 4/4 time.

Music Alphabet – First seven letters of the English alphabet.

Piano – [dynamic] Italian word meaning soft.

Quarter Note – Gets 1 beat in 4/4 time.

Whole Note – Gets 4 beats in 4/4 time.

Extra Ear Training Practice A
High or Low

If you hear high notes color the bird. If you hear low notes, color the dog.

1	2	3

If you hear high notes, color the cloud. If you hear low notes, color the flowers.

4	5	6

If you hear high notes, color the butterfly. If you hear low notes, color the ant.

7	8	9

The teacher may choose from these examples.

Extra Ear Training Practice B
Loud or Soft

If you hear loud color the roaring hippo. If you hear soft notes, color the frog.

1

2

3

If you hear loud notes, color the dog. If you hear soft notes, color the cat.

4

5

6

If you hear loud notes, color the alarm clock. If you hear soft notes, color the snow.

7

8

9

The teacher may choose from these examples add a dynamic *f* or *p*.

Extra Ear Training Practice C
Identify Open Strings

If you hear the C string, color the C house. If you hear the A string, color the A house.

1.

2.

3.

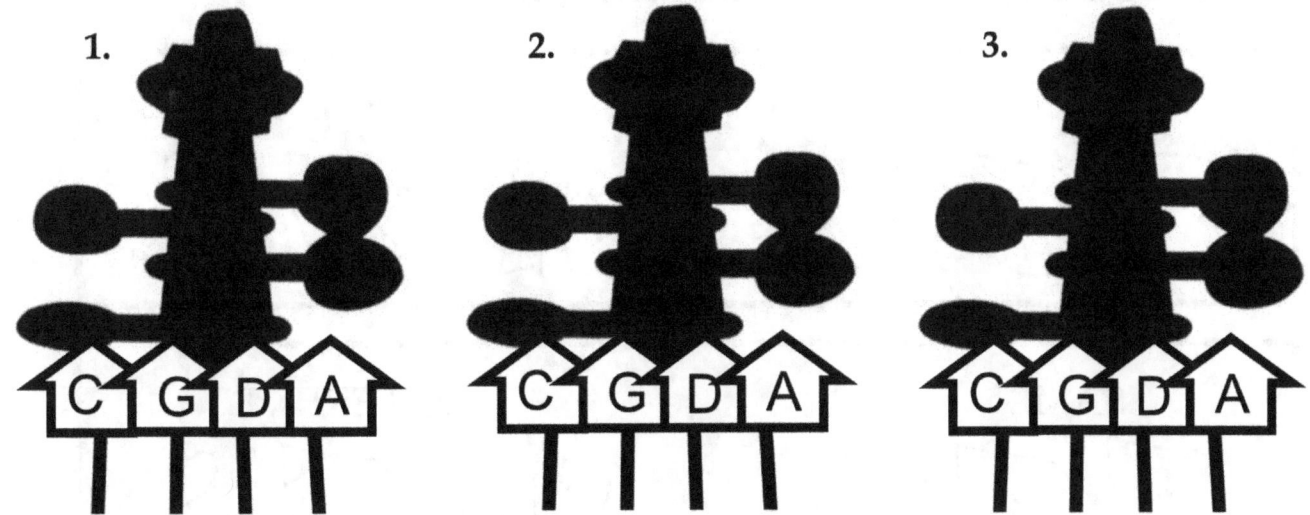

If you hear the D string, color the D house. If you hear the A string, color the A house.

4.

5.

6.

7.

8.

9.

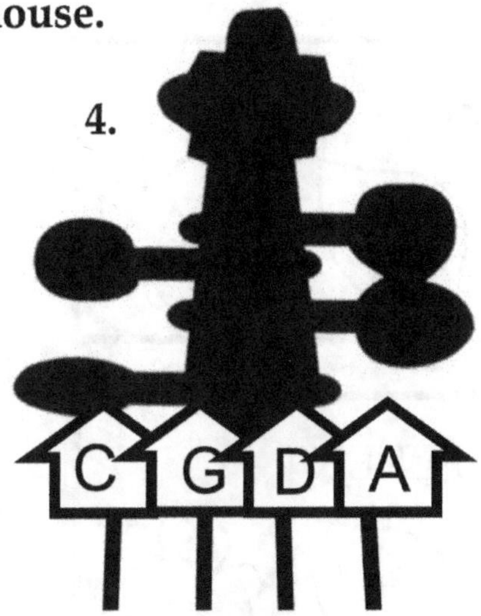

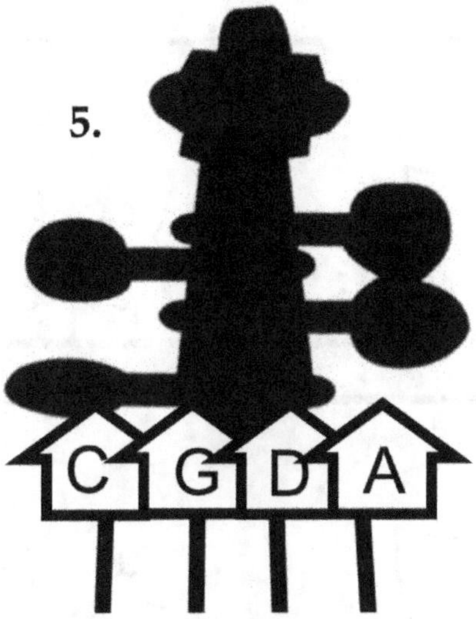

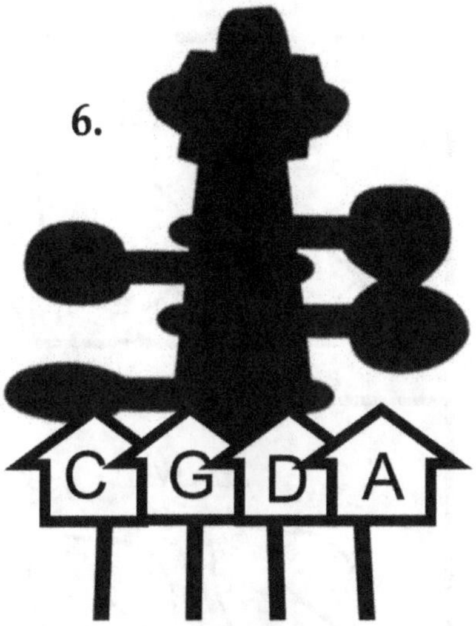

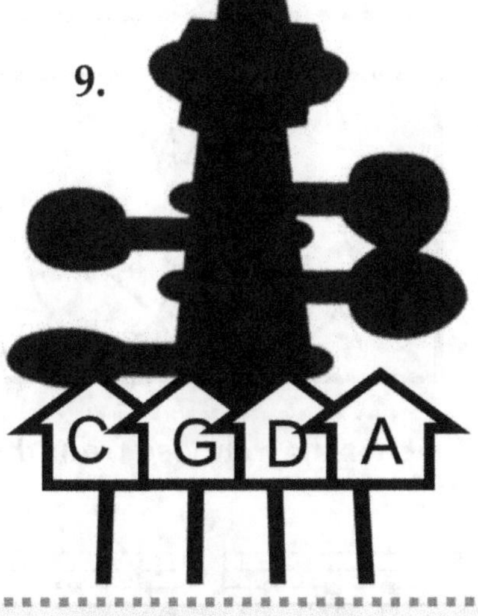

The teacher or practice partner may choose to play a rhythm pattern on an open string.

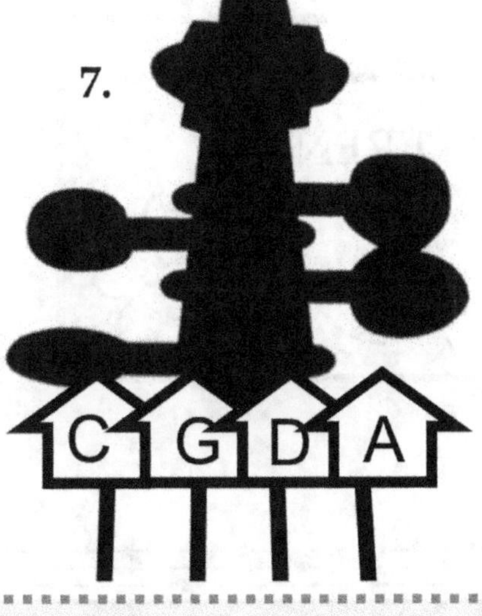

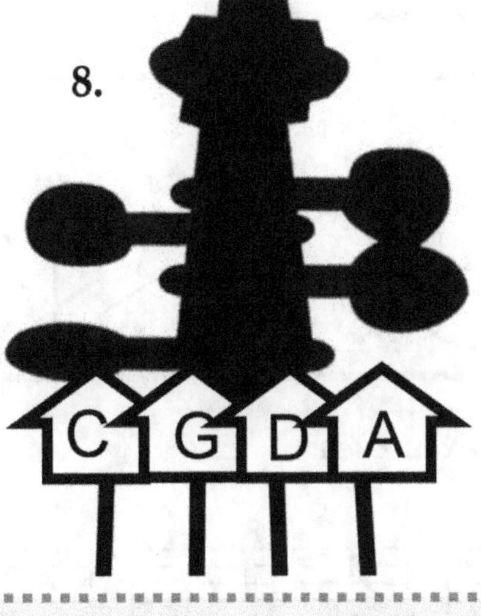

Extra Ear Training Practice D
Same or Different

If you hear the same note 3 times, color the leaves that are the same. If you hear 3 notes that are different, color the leaves that are different.

1. SAME   DIFFERENT

2. SAME   DIFFERENT

3. SAME   DIFFERENT

4. SAME   DIFFERENT

5. SAME   DIFFERENT

The teacher may choose from these examples:

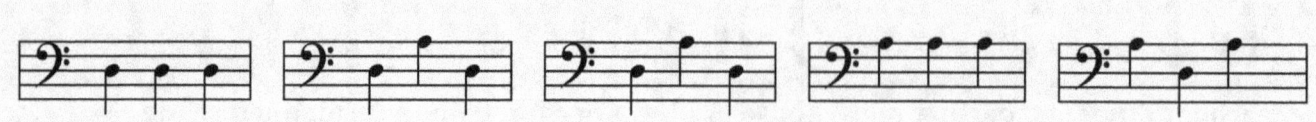

Extra Ear Training Practice E
A or E & forte or piano

Color the dolphin if you hear the D string. Color the ant if you hear the A string. Then, circle whether you hear forte or piano.

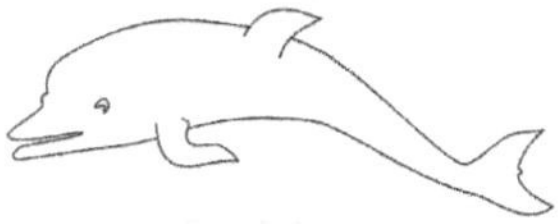

1. D string   *f* or *p*   A string

2. D string   *f* or *p*   A string

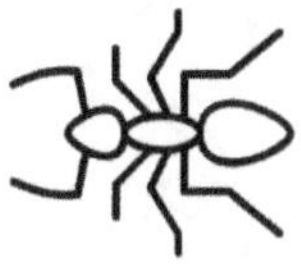

3. D string 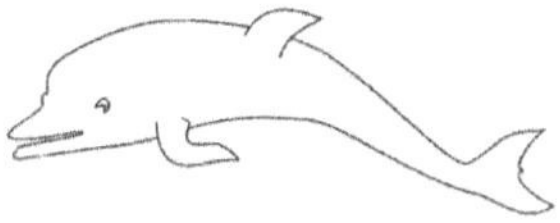   *f* or *p*   A string

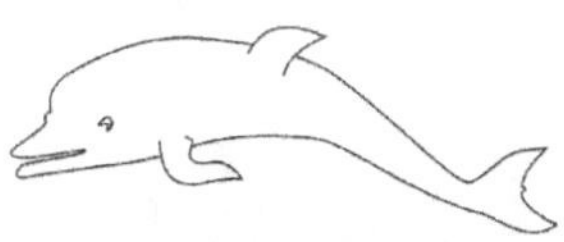

4. D string 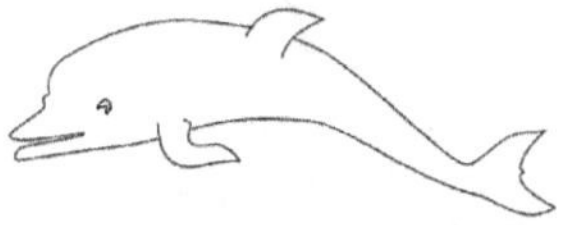   *f* or *p*   A string

5. D string 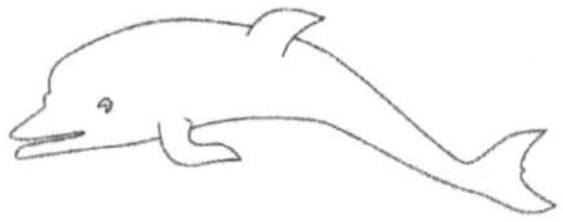   *f* or *p*   A string

Teacher can choose from these examples and choose the dynamic to play:

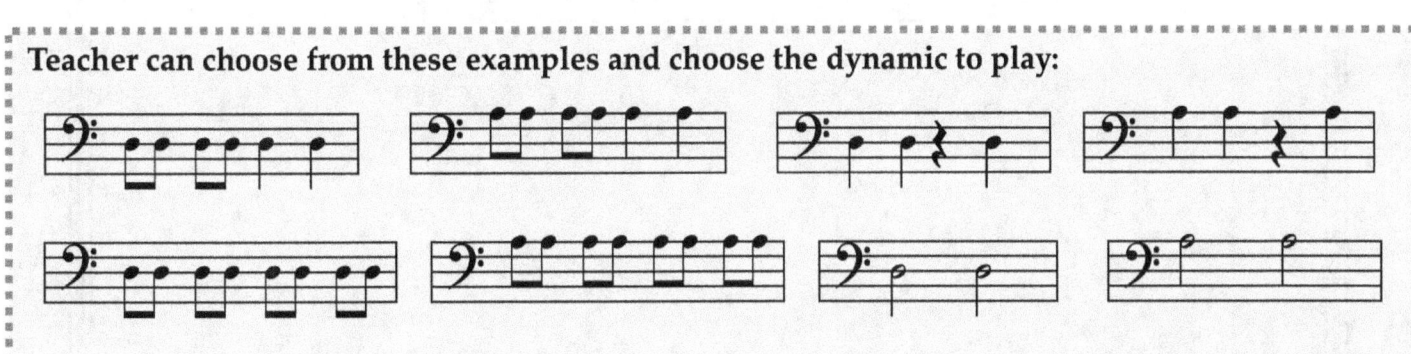

Hooray!

_____

has completed

The Magic of Music Theory
Pre-Reading A

and is now ready for Pre-Reading B

_____
(Teacher)

_____
(Date)

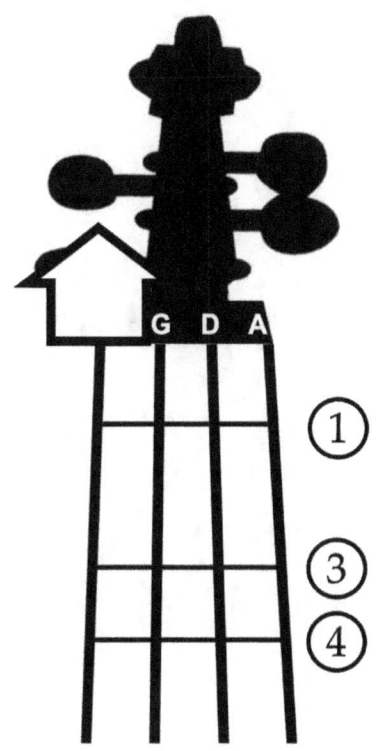

①

③

④

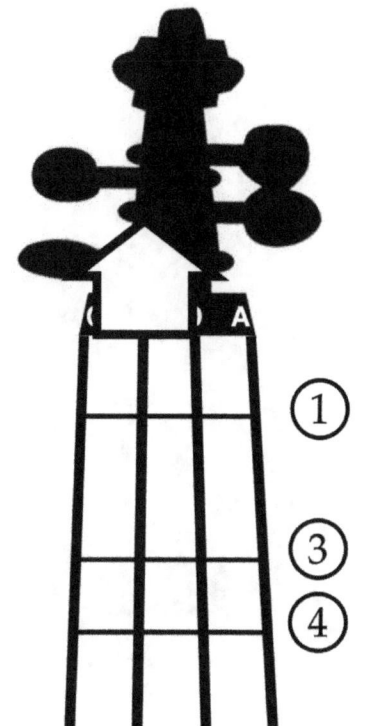

①

③

④

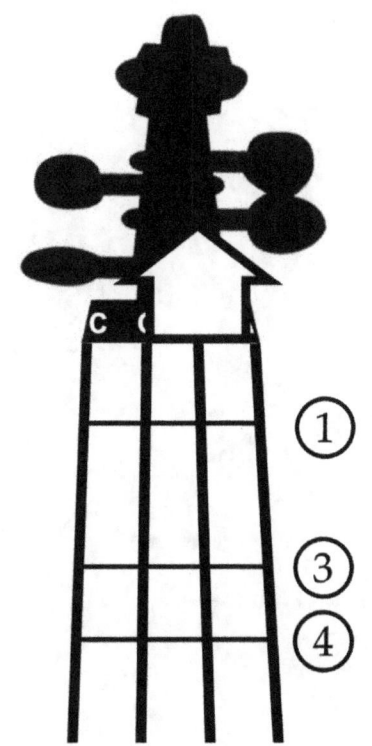

①

③

④

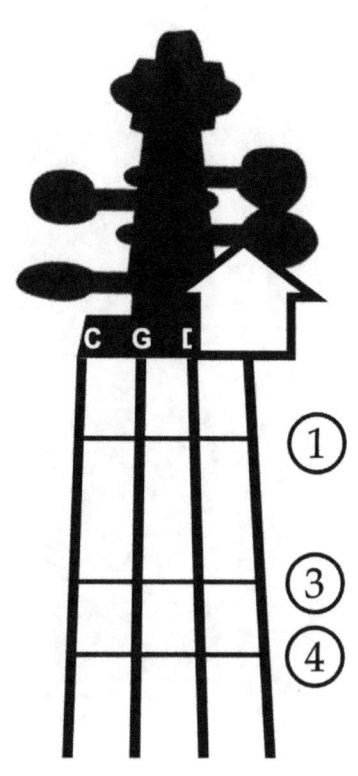

①

③

④

G

C

A

D

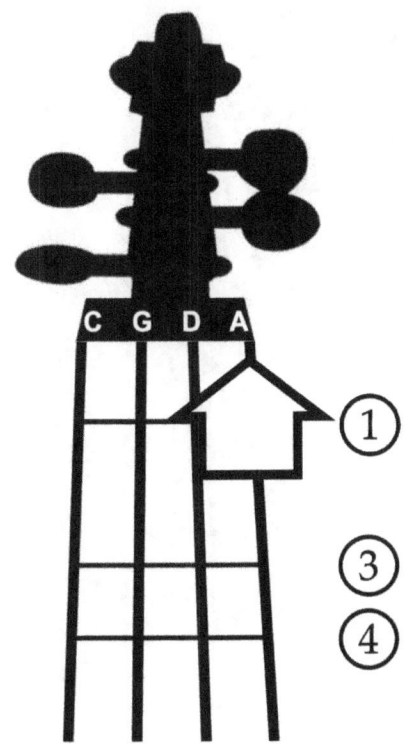

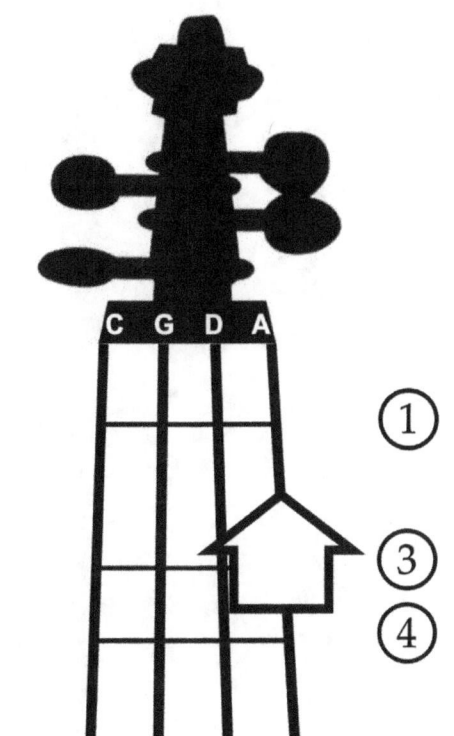

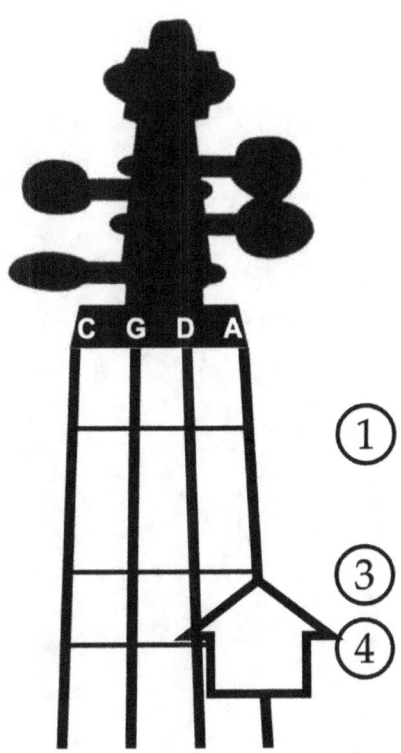

C#

B

D

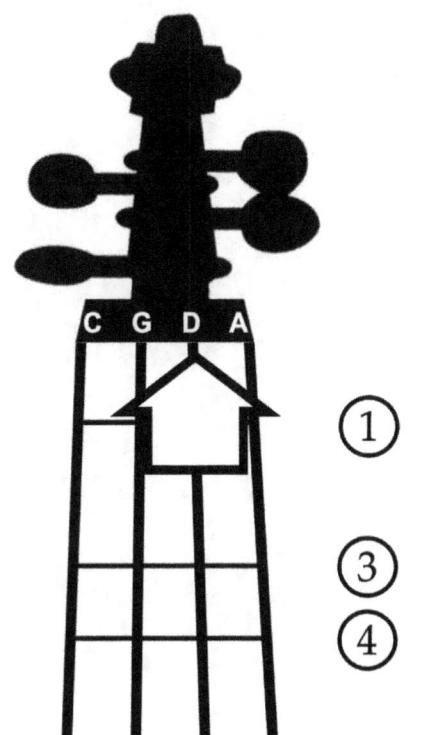

①

③

④

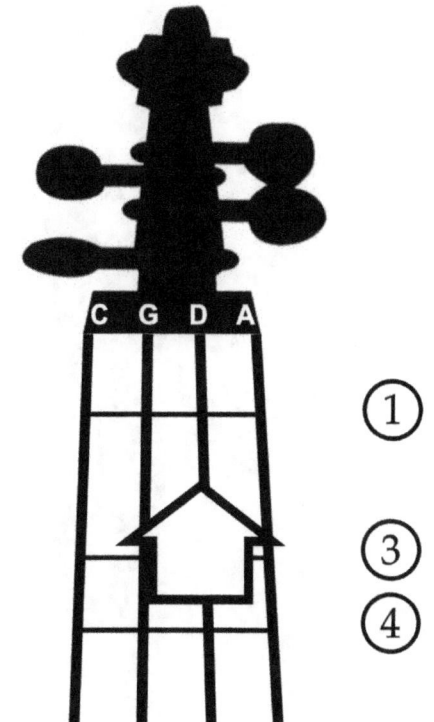

①

③

④

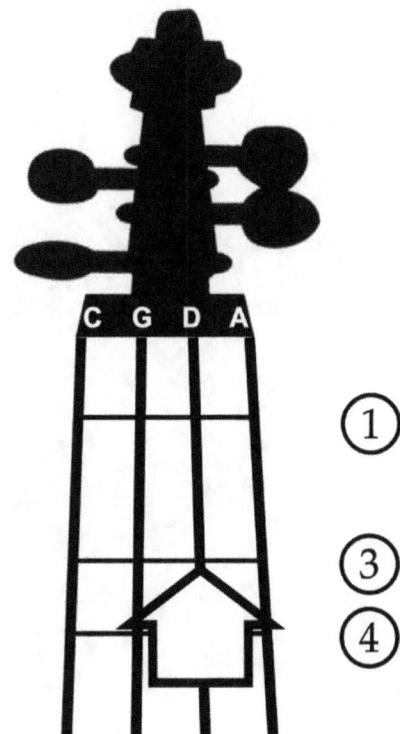

①

③

④

F#

E

G

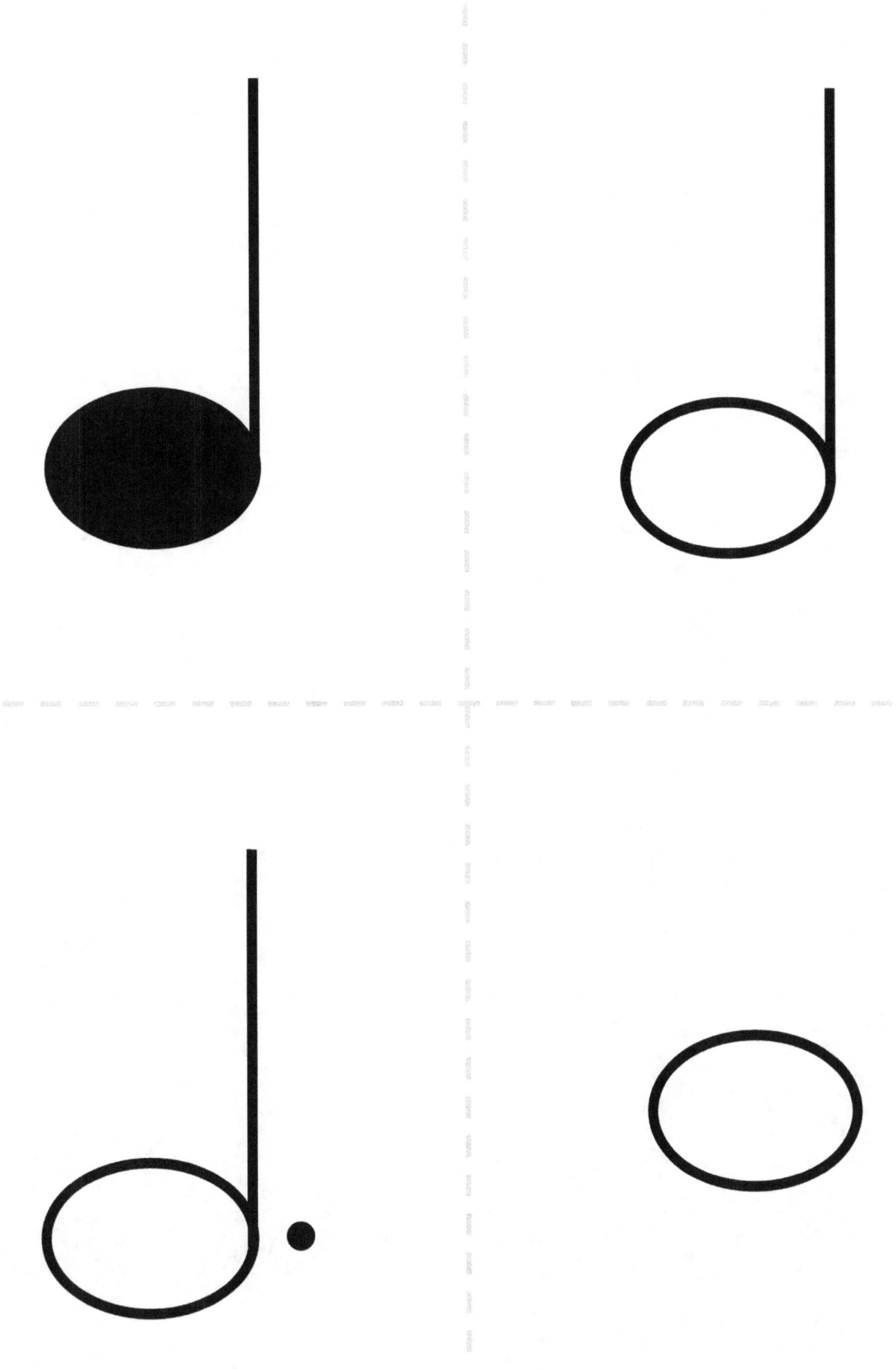

Half Note

2 Beats

Quarter Note

1 Beat

Whole Note

4 Beats

Dotted Half Note

3 Beats

www.ingramcontent.com/pod-product-compliance
Lightning Source LLC
Chambersburg PA
CBHW081007120626
46546CB00010B/3053